gardening in VANCOUVER

gardening in VANCOUVER

by
JUDY NEWTON

Technical Editor
BRIAN ANDREWS

LONE
PINE

Dedicated to my grandchildren — Ashley, Trevor, Kyle, Christopher, Colin, and James — gardeners of the future.

The Publisher:
Lone Pine Publishing
206, 10426-81 Avenue
Edmonton, Alberta, Canada
T6E 1X5

Canadian Cataloguing in Publication Data
Newton, Judy, 1940-
Gardening in .Vancouver

Includes bibliographical references and index.
ISBN 0-919433-.74-X
1. Gardening—British Columbia—Vancouver.   I. Title.

SB453.3.C2N49 1992   635'.09711'33   C92-091152-8

Technical editor: *Brian Andrews*
Editor: *Tanya Stewart*
Designer: *Beata Kurpinski*
Illustrator: *John Driedger*
Printer: *Quality Colour Press Ltd., Edmonton, Alberta, Canada*

Cover photo: *Brian Stablyk*
Back cover inset photo: *Judy Newton*

The publisher gratefully acknowledges the assistance of the Federal Department of Communications, Alberta Culture and Multiculturalism, and the Alberta Foundation for the Literary Arts in the publication of this book

All interior photographs by *Brian Andrews* except the following:
Pat Tucker: p.56 (top); p.57 (bottom); p.114 (bottom); p.117 (bottom); p.122 (bottom); p.123 (both); p.124 (bottom)
Judy Newton: p.49-52, 57(top)

CONTENTS

ACKNOWLEDGEMENTS

Books are never written in isolation. Friends, family and colleagues always make a large contribution with their advice, knowledge, moral support and humour. A special thanks to David Tarrant, who gives me the confidence to try, and Gerald Straley, whose advice I trust implicitly. Thank you to Wilf Nicholls and David Tarrant for reading the manuscript.

INTRODUCTION

Are you intrigued by stories of the old Victory Gardens but unfamiliar with gardening? Have you always wanted to add a bit of colour to your barren balcony or city block? Do you enjoy the taste of fresh vegetables in the summer but are inexperienced in raising plants? *Gardening in Vancouver* will answer your questions concerning basic methods and techniques, and will serve as a guide to planning and designing everything from ornamental lawns to window-box arrangements.

Gardening in Vancouver will also shatter a few myths. Some books on gardening give the impression that the beginner must already be familiar with complicated processes and long tables of statistics, even before planting the first seeds. Others imply that only expansive gardens on large lots are worthwhile, whereas in truth, anyone with even a small space can produce beautiful results.

Gardening in Vancouver is the second of a Canada-wide series of local gardening manuals. The beginner will find much common sense here, while the more experienced gardener may pick up some new ideas. All will benefit from the local emphasis of the book. Far too many gardening books are steeped in generalizations about "generally hardy" plants or plants "suitable for most northern locales." Every variety of flower, tree, shrub, vegetable and grass described in this book is specifically suited for the Vancouver metropolitan region. Information presented here is definitely applicable to your climate. Our series began with *Gardening in Toronto*, and additional books will soon appear for Halifax, Calgary, and other major Canadian centres.

Gardening in Vancouver is arranged in coherent, free-standing sections. The novice can start by reading the first three chapters, on Vancouver's geography and climate, basic garden planning, and soil improvement; the beginner might also take a quick look at *Chapter Ten*, which contains valuable information on controlling pests and diseases. Those with limited space will find *Chapter Four: Gardening in Small Spaces* most helpful. The remaining chapters deal with specific aspects of gardening, including fruits, vegetables, flowers, lawns, trees and shrubs, which can be read as required.

Beginners may have the impression that gardening consists of endless hours of backbreaking, unrewarding toil under the hot sun. This does not need to be true; gardening can be both rewarding and fun. A well-kept lawn, the first red apple of the season, a basket of tangy tomatoes and crisp orange carrots, even a pot of begonias on the patio all produce the same effect: satisfaction in growing something of your own and in a job well done. Use this book as a guide. Experiment with the possible combinations. Most of all, enjoy yourself.

CHAPTER 1

GEOGRAPHY & CLIMATE

The ancient landscape of Vancouver was covered with lush rainforest. Giant trees over 300 feet high towered over a panorama that is now a city. The conditions that fostered this abundance still exist in the area, providing the potential for luxuriant growth in our local gardens.

Located between the Coastal Mountains and the Strait of Georgia, Vancouver and the Lower Mainland are rich in sediments deposited by retreating glaciers and the flood waters of the Fraser River. The topography and rainfall create diverse environments throughout the area. The wash of heavy rains over the steep mountain slopes of North Vancouver has removed all but a thin layer of soil. To the south, fertile agricultural soils are found along the ancient and present-day passages of the Fraser River. Surface and subsurface drainage can vary greatly, from the fast draining northern slopes to the high water tables of Richmond. Eastward, the Fraser Estuary extends as far as Chilliwack, where the ocean tides still affect the river's flow.

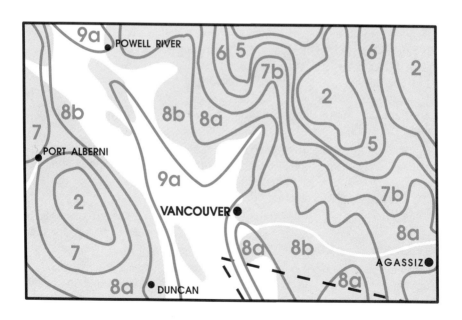

CLIMATE

The mild currents of the Pacific Ocean have a moderating effect on the climate in Vancouver, making the city a great place for gardening enthusiasts. In winter, when the water is warmer than the air, Vancouver's temperature remains mild but rather damp. In summer, the cooler water moderates the air so the days are seldom very hot.

Rainfall varies greatly, depending on how close you are to the mountains. Gardens in the southwest corner receive considerably less rain than those with their backs to the mountains. The average precipitation at the Vancouver International Airport is 1,113 mm (43.8 inches) compared to 2,695 mm (106 inches) in North Vancouver's Lynn Valley -- well over twice the precipitation. The rainfall can even vary considerably from the North Vancouver beaches, 1764 mm (60.4 inches) to the upper slopes or from one valley to the next. In general though, the higher the elevation, the greater the rainfall.

Precipitation also increases toward the eastern regions of the Fraser Valley, although not as rapidly as the transition to the north. New Westminster receives 1,580 mm (62.2 inches) and Chilliwack has 1,680 mm (74 inches). Most rainfall arrives in winter, with long dry spells from April to September.

Temperature can also vary significantly throughout Vancouver and the Lower Mainland. The mean daily temperature at the Vancouver International Airport is 2.4° C (36.6° F) in January and 17.6° C (63.7° F) in July. The distance of Chilliwack from the moderating ocean creates a greater variation with 1.5 °C in January and 18.2° C in July.

The average frost free period at the airport is from March 31 to November 3, giving about 216 frost free days. For a reporting period of 43 years, this figure varied from as low as 161 days to as high as 248 days. Areas throughout the Lower Mainland are influenced by localized microclimatic conditions. The University of British Columbia, for example, averages 244 frost free days, Kitsilano 219, West Van/Capilano 210, Ladner 163, New Westminster 234 and Chilliwack 216.

Light levels in winter are often low due to fog and cloud cover. The average amount of bright sunshine in January is just 54 hours at the airport, while July averages 307 hours. The annual average of sunshine is 1,920 hours, with April to August each receiving over 250 hours.

Wind is not usually a problem during the summer growing season, but during the winter months, storms can blow in with violent force. The effect of wind on the garden or adjacent trees will vary substantially with location and shelter.

During some winters there will be little or no snow while in other years it may stay for a week or so. Although gardens at higher elevations generally receive more snow, distribution is hard to predict. It is not uncommon for snowfall to be very heavy in one area, while a few streets over there will be almost none.

THE SEASONS

In Vancouver, spring is a long season. If the winter is mild, spring seems to start in January, but in some years, winter returns in February. Often there is a dry period in late spring, catching us by surprise. Don't forget to check plants for water during this time. Summers are often wet and cool until the beginning of July. Once the sun appears, it usually stays until September with little or no rain. By October the rains have started, interspersed with lovely sunny days. A killing frost, depending on the area, arrives in early November most years. Winter is mild in Vancouver with temperatures above freezing most days. During cold snaps there is rarely a snow cover to protect plants.

HARDINESS AND EFFECTS OF CLIMATE

Vancouver is in climatic zone 8B. The range of plants that may be grown on the West Coast is greater than in any other area of Canada. Many broad-leafed vines, ground covers, shrubs and trees grow in the area. Some of the more exotic plants are *Clematis armandii*, azaleas, rhododendrons, magnolias, Japanese flowering cherries, *Skimmia japonica* and *Jasminum nudiflorum*. Some less hardy plants that grow in protected areas are *Hebe*, *Ceanothus*, *Eucalyptus* and *Garrya*. As well as broad-leafed evergreens, there are many deciduous trees and shrubs and interesting conifers. The choice of perennials, bulbs and alpine plants has hooked many a gardener into growing more than just a few junipers and some bedding plants.

WINTER INJURY TO TREES AND SHRUBS

February seems to be the killing month in Vancouver. We may be lucky for seven or eight years and then have a winter that kills many of the borderline hardy plants. In some cases only the flower buds are affected. This may be a problem for species that bloom early in the spring or have very exposed buds. Then there are the surprises: plants like the flowering gingers that were not thought to be hardy are just fine.

SUMMARY

Vancouverites are rather smug about the climate — with good reason. We can grow a wide assortment of plants, and vegetables may be harvested most of the winter. The winters are wet but mild and the summers cool but sunny. What more could you ask for?

CHAPTER 2

GARDEN PLANNING

Planning is a creative activity. It involves anticipating future events and making decisions to accommodate them.

In any major gardening project, planning should always precede action. Planning involves deciding

- what activities are wanted in the garden
- what features the garden will contain
- how much space will be required for each activity and feature
- where the spaces for each activity and feature will be placed and in what relationship to each other
- how function and form can be integrated to result in a comfortable, easily used and beautiful garden

Answers to these and related questions will form the basis of a blueprint for the orderly and logical development of a garden, over time.

Well-conceived and drawn plans reduce errors. They save time, energy and money. This process allows mistakes to be made and corrected on paper.

The planning process begins with taking stock. This involves collecting and preparing certain kinds of information.

A DESIGN PROGRAM

Develop a well-articulated but simply written statement of design objectives: in other words, a list of all the needs and wants that you intend your garden to satisfy, how they can be accommodated in relation to site characteristics and limitations, plus the solutions to anticipated problems.

SITE PLAN

Prepare a plan, accurately drawn to scale, showing the exact location of all established features on the land surface, and those that run underground or above the site. Use various styles of broken and dotted lines to symbolize sewer, power, water and property lines, etc. A few contour lines to indicate slopes and major changes or differences in elevations should be included where appropriate. Also indicate where shade will be cast by the house, garage and any permanent trees during all seasons.

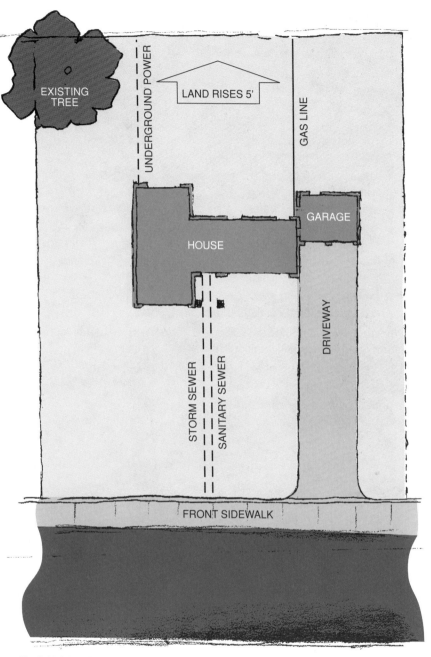

EXISTING TREE

UNDERGROUND POWER

LAND RISES 5'

GAS LINE

GARAGE

HOUSE

STORM SEWER

SANITARY SEWER

DRIVEWAY

FRONT SIDEWALK

The initial site plan should show the exact location of all established features, including those at the land surface, above the site, and underground.

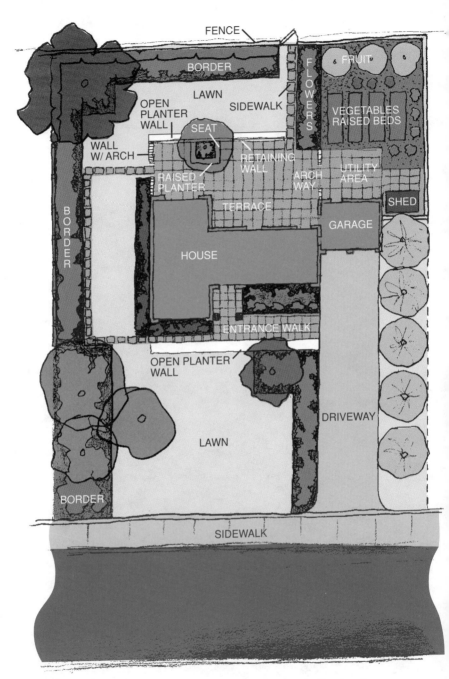

FENCE

BORDER

LAWN

OPEN PLANTER WALL

SIDEWALK

FLOWERS

FRUIT

VEGETABLES RAISED BEDS

WALL W/ ARCH

SEAT

RETAINING WALL

ARCH WAY

UTILITY AREA

BORDER

RAISED PLANTER

SHED

TERRACE

GARAGE

HOUSE

ENTRANCE WALK

OPEN PLANTER WALL

DRIVEWAY

LAWN

BORDER

SIDEWALK

The final plan includes all garden and architectural features to be developed.

OFFSITE FEATURES

Make an inventory of features, not on your site, that may affect your plans. Include pleasant and unpleasant views and vistas, and trees that may be framed by you to be visually incorporated into your landscape. Don't forget features that need to be screened. Include these items on your site plan, outside the property lines in the form of notes and arrows.

THE HOUSE

On the site plan, locate the house and note the size, shape and elevations of all rooms, windows, doors, decks, steps and floors. Make notes describing the views from windows and doors.

BASIC LANDSCAPE USES

Using the collected information, group together the various proposed functions and their related spaces into the four basic landscape categories: Public, Private, Family and Service Areas. Decide where they should be located on the site. It's very similar to designing the floor plan of a house. Ensure that each group of uses relates logically to the others, and avoid conflicts. Bear in mind that the final result should be functional and beautiful.

BASIC DESIGN PRINCIPLES

The following are basic principles that should be appreciated by the garden planner:

Definition Outdoor spaces and garden features should be defined. This may be achieved by simple lines at ground level, for example the edges of lawns or patios, a pathway, or a wall, fence, screen, hedge, border or row of trees.

Enclosure Outdoor spaces or rooms will often be enclosed, partially or fully, using hedges, borders of plants, walls, fences, screens, rows of trees or shrubs, or flower beds, etc.

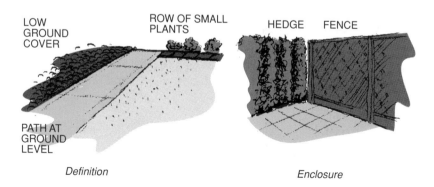

Definition   *Enclosure*

Outdoor spaces and garden features may be either defined or enclosed. Enclosure always creates definition, but the reverse is not true.

There is a relationship between definition and enclosure. By necessity, enclosure always creates definition but the reverse is not true. For example, a line of bricks at ground level creates definition but not enclosure, whereas a hedge or wall creates both.

Circulation   Always provide logical, easy and comfortable circulation between and within the various spaces and features of a garden for both people and, where appropriate, vehicles.

Utility and Beauty   Pursue the principle that good landscape planning and design is both functional and beautiful -- that these two objectives can be integrated.

LOCATION AND PLACEMENT

Here are a few practical considerations to consider when locating various crops, plants and features.

VEGETABLES

Site   The site should be as level as possible, open and sunny, receiving at least 8 hours of direct sunlight each day during mid-summer and sheltered from prevailing winds.

Orientation   In the Vancouver area, rows generally run north and south.

Definition   Vegetables should be defined and preferably separated from the rest of the garden by a live or architectural screen.

TREE FRUITS

Site   Fruit trees need to be planted on well drained soil that does not become waterlogged in the winter. Fruit trees should receive full sun.

Orientation   When fruit trees are planted in rows they are usually oriented in a north/south direction.

Protection   Fruit trees do not need winter protection in the Vancouver area.

Definition   An orchard or fruit garden may be defined and screened from, or be visually integrated with, other areas of the garden, depending on the specific layout and the designer's intention and preference.

SMALL FRUITS

Site   Small fruits will grow in areas that are too wet for the deeper rooted fruit trees. Small fruits require full sun.

Orientation   Small fruits are planted in a north/south orientation.

Protection   Small fruits do not require winter protection.

TREES AND SHRUBS

Trees and shrubs may be used in a wide variety of locations depending on their individual preferences for aspect, sun and shade. Typical uses include:

- single specimens in lawns, beds, borders, planters and planting holes in paved areas
- small groups in beds and borders
- groves to create naturalistic settings
- lines: the plants widely spaced to create tall, open intermittent screens and loose hedges; or closely spaced to create dense, tall and medium hedges
- components of windbreaks

The following factors should be taken into account when planning the placement of trees and shrubs:

Size at Maturity   Sufficient space must be provided to allow woody plants to grow and achieve mature size and the designer's intended effect. Find out the expected height and spread at maturity. (See Size and Form at Maturity, Chapter 8.)

Form   Woody plants have a characteristic shape or form which may be similar throughout the life of a plant or change with its age.

Texture   Texture is largely determined by the density of the branch, twig structure and size of leaves. Plants with widely spaced, large leaves are said to be "coarse" textured, while those with densely distributed, small leaves are described as "fine" textured.

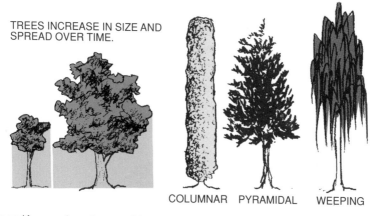

TREES INCREASE IN SIZE AND SPREAD OVER TIME.

COLUMNAR   PYRAMIDAL   WEEPING

Size and form are important considerations when planning the location of trees and shrubs in the garden.

Foliage Colour   Both summer and winter foliage are important long-term design values. Frequently seen colours include reddish-purple, yellow, silvery or grey, white or yellow variegated and various shades of green.

Flowers   Colour, form, texture and time of flowering are important considerations.

Bark   An important element of colour and texture, particularly during winter.

Fruit   Adds a source of colour in late summer, autumn and early winter.

Autumn Colour   Provides a final blaze of colour at the close of the growing season.

Winter Colour   Foliage, bark and berries are not the only winter colour in the landscape. Several trees and shrubs bloom in the winter or have attractive buds throughout the winter. Examples are *Corylopsis sinensis, Stachyurus chinensis, Garrya eliptica* —the most unusual types— and *Pieris japonica* and *Skimmia japonica*.

HERBACEOUS PERENNIALS

See Chapter 6 for a definition of these lovely plants.

Herbaceous perennials may be planted alone or mixed with shrubs and annuals in beds, borders and planters. Other uses include:

- the time honoured classic "herbaceous border" containing a wide variety of herbaceous perennials and sometimes annuals, particularly towards the front. Variations on the theme include spring and fall flowering borders and those featuring specific colour schemes such as purple-mauve flowers, or white flowers and silvery foliage,
- in combination with shrubs and annuals in mixed borders,
- shade-loving and shade-tolerant kinds: very appropriate and attractive in woodland gardens and shady areas,
- several that make excellent summer ground covers.

Orientation   Except shade-loving and shade-tolerant types, most herbaceous perennials prefer open, sunny locations, protected from wind. Gentle, north-facing slopes, protected from winter winds, make excellent environments. Locations on the north side of a house, fence or wall, just beyond the area shaded during mid-summer, are also good spots.

Design Characteristics   As discussed for "Trees and Shrubs," size, form, texture, foliage colour, and flower colour and timing are important in the selection and location of perennials.

ANNUALS

Season of Bloom   Annuals are unique. They have the longest season of bloom. Except for plants with coloured foliage, they provide the longest period of colour during the growing season.

Uses   Like herbaceous perennials, they may be used in a variety of ways in both sunny and shady locations. Their major contribution to garden design is the provision of splashes and highlights of strong, bright, long-term colour. In addition to beds and borders, plant them in pots, urns, tubs and planters.

Design Characteristics   Although design characteristics are similar to other plants, due to their strong colours and the common practice of close spacing and massed planting, height and colour of annuals are the major design considerations.

GROUND COVERS

Uses   As the name suggests, these are plants or inert materials that cover the surface of the ground. Inert kinds include gravel, shale, pebbles, crushed rock, marble chips and bark, etc., placed directly on the ground, landscape fabrics or perforated plastic sheets.

There is a wide range of ground covering evergreen and deciduous shrubs as well as herbaceous perennials and annuals.

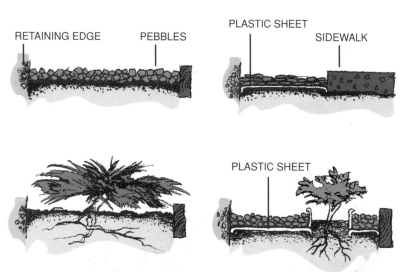

Various combinations of plants and inert materials may be used as ground covers in areas of high traffic, where plants are difficult to grow, to create interesting surfaces, and for many other purposes.

Inert groundcovers are used
- where plants are impossible or too difficult to grow.
- in areas of high traffic
- to reduce or minimize the use of plants and thereby maintenance
- to create surfaces of interesting colour and texture, contrasting or harmonizing with lawns, decks, paved areas and other surfaces
- as mulches for live plantings

In addition to some of the above uses, live covers are used to
- link groups of shrubs and perennials in planting arrangements
- create interesting live carpets and tapestries using texture, colour and form
- cover areas where grass will not grow
- cover slopes, banks, mounds, odd shaped areas and shady places where mowing and other maintenance is difficult

VINES

Depending on their species characteristics, vines may be used as climbers, trailers or ground covers. Climbers and trailers will climb up or trail over and down walls, fences, slopes, trees and shrubs, pillars, pergolas, trellises and other supports. Screens of various densities can be developed and ugly features hidden.

Vines are excellent for creating vertical accents and delicate traceries on walls, fences, screens and arches, providing interesting and welcome contrasts of form.

Vines can add colour and texture to an ordinary fence, and create a visually appealing archway.

BULBS, CORMS AND TUBERS

Many kinds of hardy and tender plants with underground bulbs, corms, tubers and tuberous roots may be grown, adding to the gardener's palette. For planning and design purposes they may be considered in the same light as herbaceous perennials and annuals. However, several kinds have additional, significant characteristics: some flower early or late in the season, and others are upright or arching, with sword shaped, grass-like or narrow foliage, resulting in strong or distinctive forms.

PLANTING ON SLOPES.

Unless special provisions are made for irrigation and surface soil stabilization, the maximum recommended slope for a "planted bank" is just over one vertical to two horizontal or a 26 per cent grade.

LAWNS

Orientation   Most lawns require an open, sunny location since many grasses are not shade-tolerant. If lawns are desired in shaded areas, shade-tolerant grasses must be selected.

Limitations on Levels   When locating a lawn on a site, bear in mind the following limitations:
- minimum surface slope is
  - a) 1 in 100 on well drained soils
  - b) 2 in 100 on poorly drained soils
- avoid slopes greater than 15 in 100
- maximum mowable slope is 1 in 3

On slopes that are too steep to mow, the development of terraces is strongly recommended. Wherever possible, use terraces to take advantage of differences in elevation to add visual interest to a landscape.

Design Characteristics   In addition to forming the basic carpet in a garden, lawns provide a verdant background and a universal foil to all garden features and plants.

ARCHITECTURAL FEATURES

It is unlikely that any urban gardens can be satisfactorily developed without some "hard landscape" and architectural features. While pathways, driveways, front and back steps, and paved "patios" are commonly included, less obvious features are often overlooked.

TERRACES AND DECKS

Terraced lawns have been previously mentioned. Paved terraces, retained by walls or linked by slopes to lawns, other paved areas or borders are very functional, interesting and beautiful features.

WALLS

These strong elements of design may be tall walls, providing a strong sense of enclosure, protection and warmth; retaining walls of various sizes, holding back the soil or supporting terraces; walls of smaller stature, used to define garden spaces and planting areas; open top walls, used as planters in their own right.

SCREENS, FENCES, TRELLISES, PERGOLAS AND ARCHES

All are used to define and enclose garden spaces, paths, driveways and features, and support plants.

STEPS

These are an often neglected element in the garden, yet they represent golden opportunities for creating beautiful design features. There are endless variations on the theme when using them to bridge differences in elevation.

PAVED AREAS

In addition to the traditional concrete and interlocking bricks there are many interesting and beautiful paving materials available, including gravel, crushed rock, shale, asphalt, bricks, natural and manufactured paving blocks, wooden blocks, cross-sections of tree trunks, and several proprietary products.

Don't forget that besides the customary "patio" for a few drinks and a barbecue, there are other outdoor spaces, particularly those receiving hard pedestrian use, where paving makes good sense.

Steps can be used to add beauty to the landscape of the garden while serving the more practical purpose of bridging differences in elevation.

STATUARY, SCULPTURE, AND STONE FEATURES

These elements can add much interest, beauty and variety of form to a garden. As points of interest or focal points to terminate vistas, paths and strong lines of sight, they play an important role in garden design and exterior decoration. They are also very attractive when associated with walls, paved areas and lawns.

GAZEBOS AND SUMMER HOUSES

These are attractive and functional additions to a garden, and are very useful for outdoor entertaining and shelter in wet weather.

GREENHOUSES

If you plan eventually to have a greenhouse, be sure to provide space for it in a location where there will be plenty of unobstructed sunlight. Locate it in relation to the other service functions in the garden, unless you plan to use it as an architectural feature.

SHEDS

These are very useful for storing lawnmowers, tools, garden furniture and fertilizers etc. If you don't plan to build immediately, location and space should be indicated on original plans.

FOUNTAINS AND POOLS

Visually, these play a similar role to statuary and sculpture but add the value of movement through the use of spraying, falling and running water. The sound of rippling and splashing water, reflection of light and the tranquility of a still pool provide additional dimensions.

SPECIAL GARDEN FEATURES

When planning, in addition to the kinds of functional outdoor spaces or rooms previously described, bear in mind that for the specialist, hobbyist and just generally enthusiastic gardener, there are several types of garden that may be specially featured as a part of a garden or even be used as its general theme.

ROCK GARDENS

These require open, sunny locations, exposed to the south or south-west, away from the roots and overhanging canopies of trees. While gentle slopes are ideal, with careful design and construction flat areas can be satisfactory. Perfect drainage is a must.

WATER AND BOG GARDENS

Usually less formal than pools, they can be naturalistic ponds and streams, plus waterfalls of various scales, with related marginal and wetland areas. Generally, they require sunny to semi-shaded locations but not heavily shaded areas. If streams are to be featured, slightly-sloping land is the easiest to develop.

Streams, pools and bogs associate well with rock gardens, providing drainage for the latter is not compromised.

WOODLAND GARDENS

These types of gardens provide naturalistic woodland settings, containing sunny, semi-shaded, and more heavily shaded areas to accommodate a wide variety of plants, many of which prefer a relatively shady environment.

An ideal site will be naturally wooded or contain an adequate number of more mature planted trees, and provide a variety of micro-environments. There should be sufficient trees to allow immediate plantings of woodland plants. Inter-planting with new trees will facilitate the development of additional, future environments.

WILD GARDENS

Very appealing gardens, approaching wild landscapes, can be created with minimal land development. They may contain elements of rock, water, bog and woodland gardens. Meadows, marshes and prairies may comprise all or just a part of a wild garden.

Development is restricted to naturalistic paths, related access facilities, and plantings of native and allied introduced plants, supplementing existing vegetation.

Perfect drainage is necessary for rock gardens, which must be located away from the roots and overhanging branches of trees.

While there is little to be done to make significant, permanent changes to the climate, there are a few time proven methods of achieving a degree of control and modification.

WIND

Windbreaks, walls, fences, screens, hedges, and shrub borders all help to break the force of wind. In general, the height of a screen determines the size of the area protected on the sheltered side (about twenty times its height). Density determines the pattern and degree of turbulence on the sheltered side. Wind screens that break the force of the wind but allow some to pass through are best. They provide a large area of protection with minimal turbulence problems.

TEMPERATURE

Wind screens also help to increase temperatures on their sheltered side. Radiant heat from walls, fences and paved areas can significantly increase temperatures in their immediate vicinity.

Cooling can be achieved by planting trees and shrubs, and the use of architectural features such as walls, screens and trellises to provide shade. Water features also have a cooling effect, both physically and psychologically, but may increase local humidity.

SUN AND SHADE

The garden planner should judge the angle and path of the sun in winter, summer, spring and fall. Exact information may be obtained from the local office of Environment Canada. Using this data, patterns of shade, cast by existing and proposed, live and architectural features can be plotted. This makes it possible to:

- plan the location of sunny and shady areas
- provide for protection from sun (for example in late evening, low angled sun may shine directly into the eyes of a person sitting on the patio)
- determine the kinds of plants for various areas

FROST PROTECTION

The main approach is to avoid placing the house, fruit and vegetable gardens, early flowering and late maturing plants, and less hardy plants, in frost pockets. These are low lying areas that collect and hold cold air. Always remember that cold air is heavier than warm, and flows down hill. Beware of placing solid fences or hedges that are densely twigged from top to bottom across a slope. The cold air will build up and pool against the barrier. Always provide adequate openings in the barrier or at its base to allow for unimpeded flow of cold air down the slope.

NOISE

Basically, noise may be controlled by the same methods as wind. Solid barriers, however, are best. While it may be romantic to believe that nature has provided we mortals with the ideal noise barrier in the form of trees, it really isn't so. While trees undoubtedly provide a measure of noise absorption and control, it's tall, man-made, solid walls that do the best job.

ATTRACTING BIRDS

Generally it is not necessary to take special action to attract birds. Once a garden reaches a reasonable level of maturity, birds that are locally abundant will visit and often nest. This requires a patient attitude. For gardeners in a bit of a hurry or who wish to attract specific kinds of birds, here are a few ideas:

- plant evergreen and deciduous trees, and some densely-twigged shrubs to provide a variety of nesting habits. Provide a variety of nesting boxes that are appropriately designed to attract local or uncommon species
- use plants that produce abundant berries, nuts and seeds
- keep insect control to the minimum, consistent with your gardening objectives and the garden's survival
- provide water for drinking and bathing
- establish feeding stations for resident species, particularly in winter
- with regard to the foregoing points, be sure to consult people in local wildlife associations

CHAPTER 3

BASIC SOIL IMPROVEMENT

In this chapter the improvement of soils is emphasized. Gardeners who are interested in a quick review of the basic principles which underlie soil improvement may wish to read "The Background to Soil Improvement" at the end of this chapter.

The best soils for gardening are loams. They are mixtures of clay, silt and sand. Composition ranges from 5 to 20 per cent clay and 20 to 60 per cent sand, with silt making up the balance. For gardening purposes they are called clayey, silty and sandy loams, depending on which material predominates. The ideal, often elusive, "medium loam" is a soil not dominated by clay, silt or sand. Its mineral content is made up of approximately 20 per cent, clay, 40 per cent silt, and 40 per cent, coarse sand, plus a generous amount of organic matter and humus. Such a soil doesn't have the extreme characteristics of clay and sand. It is well drained, easy to work and well aerated, containing adequate water and plenty of plant foods.

There are three fundamental techniques used to improve soils: drainage, tillage and the addition of soil improving materials.

DRAINAGE

Soils with high water tables are continually wet, holding water for long periods after rain and snow thaw or where surface water takes a long time to drain away. Providing adequate drainage is the first step in soil improvement.

Surface drainage is usually a function of the slope of the land. Provided the soil is permeable and overlies a well-drained subsoil, it is not normally a serious problem in most well planned and engineered urban sub-divisions.

Where the top soil overlies an impervious subsoil or the subsoil itself is saturated, a drainage scheme may be needed.

The fundamental principle of drainage is that water flows downhill and seeks its own level. Land drainage may involve using one or more of three general techniques.

Collection   Surplus water must be collected.

Transportation   It must be transported away from the affected site to a disposal site.

Disposal   It must be disposed of in a satisfactory manner.

Gardener's drainage methods include:

- Digging one or two spits (spade-depths) deep to break impermeable soil layers or hard-pans and improve porosity. Where practical this method may eliminate collection and facilitate transportation and disposal in an easy, downward manner.
- Soakaways. Large, deep holes are lined with non-cemented bricks and filled with broken bricks, rubble and coarse gravel to within 18-24 inches (45-60 cm) of ground level. A layer of medium gravel is then placed, covered by tar paper or coarse peat, then top soil. These structures will drain the immediate, surrounding area, holding the water until it gradually drains away. They may also be used as a disposal pit for water transported from elsewhere.
- Gravel Filled Trenches. Flat-bottomed trenches with sloping sides are dug approximately half a metre deep. A foot of coarse gravel is placed in the bottom and covered with 9-12 inches (22.5-30 cm) of top soil. These may act as mini-soakaways or serve to collect and transport water.
- Serious problems may require agricultural tile drains laid in trenches, bedded on and covered with gravel, then covered with top soil. These collect and transport water to a lower lying pond, creek, lake, dry well, ditch or other place for disposal.

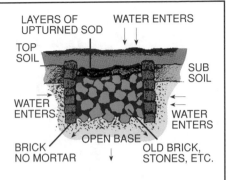

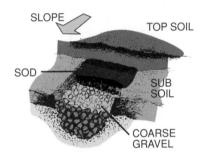

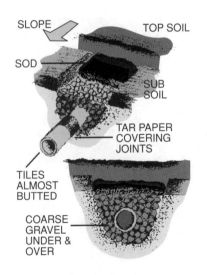

The major method of improvement is turning over the soil, adding soil improvement materials including organic matter, gritty materials and fertilizers, and thoroughly mixing them with the soil.

Digging may be accomplished mechanically or by hand. Here, time-honoured hand methods of single and double digging are described. They can readily be adapted to mechanical means, using a roto-tiller.

SINGLE DIGGING

The objective is to turn over and break up the soil, one spit deep, and thoroughly mix in the improvement materials.

As a simple example, digging a rectangular plot is described.

- Using a garden line, divide the plot into two equal halves — A and B.
- Mark a trench, 15 inches (37.5 cm) wide, across one end of Half-A.
- Using a square-nosed garden spade, dig out the top soil a full spade's depth, leaving a straight sided, flat bottom trench. Place excavated soil in a pile just outside the end of Half - B. Mark a second 15 inch (37.5 cm) wide trench behind the first.
- Dig the soil from this second trench, throwing it forward into and filling the first trench. Be sure that every crumb of soil is moved. Due to expansion the soil in the first trench will be higher than the surrounding land.
- Continue working backwards, down Half-A, trench by trench until the end of the plot is reached.
- Take out the next trench, adjacent, on Half-B, placing the soil into the last trench of Half-A.
- Continue digging, Half-B, trench by trench as previously described.
- Fill in the final trench on Half-B with the pile of soil dug from the first trench of Half-A.

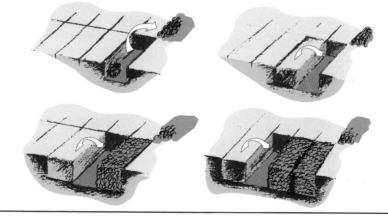

DOUBLE DIGGING

The objective is to turn over and break up the soil two spits deep, keeping the two spits or top soil and subsoil unmixed, leaving them in their respective horizons.

Although labour intensive, it is an excellent method for
- breaking new ground, especially undisturbed pasture
- initial preparation for permanent beds and borders of trees and shrubs, herbaceous perennials, fruits, asparagus and rhubarb
- breaking an impervious layer, hard-pan or badly-drained subsoil below the top soil

The general method is similar to single digging with the following changes
- use a 24 inch (60 cm) wide trench
- after digging out the top soil, fork over and break up the bottom of the trench (subsoil) a spit deep, before turning over the top soil from the next trench into it

On shallow top soils, double digging allows for the removal of some subsoil and its replacement with top soil. It may also be used to lower the elevation of an area by removing subsoil from under the top soil.

Both methods of digging allow for the incorporation of organic matter and other soil improvement materials. Simply spread the material over the soil surface prior to digging. Scatter it over the soil during digging, covering it with soil as work proceeds.

TIMING

The best time to dig is late fall. Soil can be turned over in large lumps without breaking them, leaving the lumps exposed to the beneficial cleansing and pulverizing effects of rain, snow, and freeze and thaw cycles for several months. Since most soils expand about 20-25 per cent when dug, fall digging also allows the longest time for the soil to settle. This is particularly important when land is double dug. Furthermore, cool weather makes the task easier on the digger.

When digging in spring, unless carried out early enough for natural settlement to occur, it may be necessary to lightly consolidate the soil prior to planting or seeding. Walking over the soil on the heels in closely spaced rows or one or two heavy waterings will do the job. When double digging, be sure to consolidate the lower spit after forking it over, before covering with top soil.

Never dig or cultivate soil when it is wet. This is of paramount importance on clay-dominated soils. Compressing wet soil will destroy crumb structure, porosity and air holding capacity, and impede local drainage.

SOIL AMENDMENTS

Several organic and inorganic materials are used to improve soils.

ANIMAL MANURES

Bulky, fresh or near-fresh, strawy, farmyard or stable manures should not be used just prior to planting or seeding since they may burn roots. Heavy applications may be safely made on open land in late fall.

For most uses, sweet smelling, easily crumbled, non-sticky, well-rotted manures are best and may be safely applied at any time.

Reasonably dry, crumbly, easy to handle, fresh cow manure is an excellent source of organic matter.

Sheep, chicken and pig manures are best when dried, crumbled and used as organic fertilizers or to make liquid fertilizers.

COMPOST

When well-rotted, reasonably dry, non-slimy, and crumbly-flaky, compost is an excellent source of organic matter.

PEAT MOSS

Pure, sterilized, fibrous, sphagnum peat is first class. While it contains little immediately-available plant foods, it is an excellent form of slow-decomposing, long lasting, water retaining, organic matter that has a long-term, beneficial effect on soil structure. It is a valuable additive in lawn construction, and the preparation of permanent, long-term plantings of trees, shrubs and herbaceous perennials.

Since peat moss is a semi-raw form of organic matter, during decomposition the soil organisms use much of the available nitrogen in the soil. It is therefore necessary to add a nitrogen fertilizer to the soil to compensate.

RAW FORMS

Non-resinous, small-size wood chips and sawdust, chopped straw, hay and similar forms of raw organic matter may be used. Like peat moss, they break down slowly using available nitrogen, for which compensation must be made.

GREEN MANURES

Leafy-green crops such as Fall rye, Austrian Winter pea, Winter wheat and crimson clover are sown between August 15 and the end of September and dug under several weeks before planting the garden. Extra nitrogen is not usually needed. The green manure crop will sop up the available nutrients before the winter rains have a chance to leach them out.

GRAVEL AND SAND

Fine, washed gravels up to half a centimetre across and coarse, angular particle sands with most grains between 1/16 and 1/8 inch (15 and 30 mm) may be used to improve the porosity, drainage and structure of clay soils. They must be thoroughly mixed with the clay to be effective. Bear in mind that large quantities may be required to make a noticeable improvement in porosity and texture. Remember, an ideal loam contains about 20 per cent clay and 40 per cent coarse sand. Don't use round-particle sands unless they are very coarse. Beware of very fine builder's sands; when they are mixed with clay, an intractable form of concrete results.

VERMICULITE AND PERLITE

Although not commonly used outdoors, such products may be used to improve porosity and help lighten heavy soils but may prove to be expensive where large quantities are involved.

LIME

The addition of lime will reduce soil acidity or "sweeten" sour soils. It is mostly used in the forms of agricultural lime or dolomitic lime. The dolomite lime has the advantage of supplying calcium and magnesium as well. Soil pH measures how acidic or alkaline the soil solution is and it is measured on a pH scale which ranges from 0 to 14. In high rainfall areas like Vancouver the soil is acidic and it registers lower than the neutral 7 on the scale.

Soil testing is the most dependable way to determine if a soil needs lime and how much.

SULPHUR AND ALUMINUM SULPHATE

These chemicals are used to increase the acidity of soils. Testing is also advised.

Aluminum sulphate is also used to "blue" the flowers of the common florist's hydrangea.

FORKING

A steel-tined digging fork is used to lightly turn over the top three to six inches (7.5 to 15 cm) of soil, breaking down the lumps to a finer texture, and to mix in soil amendments. Forking is an important step, prior to raking, when preparing a seed bed.

A fork is also used to break up the soil surface between permanent plants in beds and borders to aerate the soil and mix in mulches and fertilizers.

RAKING

Use a steel rake to break down the top one to two inches (2.5 to 5 cm) of the soil surface into small granules. It is also used to gather and remove stones and debris from the soil surface.

HOEING

Use a hoe to break the soil crust and develop a shallow layer of fine soil or dust mulch to reduce water loss by evaporation.

Also use it to chop off weeds just below soil level, cultivate shallowly and draw soil or "earth up" around the base of plants.

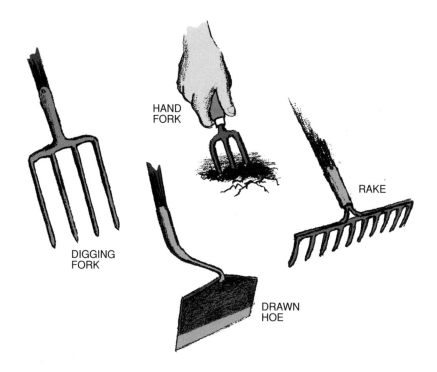

HAND FORK

RAKE

DIGGING FORK

DRAWN HOE

MULCHING

Mulching involves the application of a shallow layer of organic matter to the soil surface to conserve moisture, keep the soil cool, and smother weeds and prevent their germination. Mulching also provides a mild feed. When forked into the soil the mulch increases the organic matter content.

WATERING

To apply water to a plant's root system, the general rule is to water slowly and copiously, penetrating the soil deeply when needed, but leaving as long an interval as practical between waterings. This will encourage deep rooting and drought tolerance. The main exception is when germinating seeds. Seed beds, newly-sown lawns and rows of seeds should be watered frequently and lightly with shallow penetration, without disturbing the soil surface until germination occurs. After sprouting, gradually increase the amount of water per application and decrease the frequency of application until the general rule is reinstated.

SEEDBED PREPARATION

Dig, and if required, manure the plot. If fall digging is practised, the addition of fertilizer is left until spring. Fork over the plot to break down lumps and mix in the manure and fertilizer. Finally, rake and cross-rake to develop a level, 1.5 to 2 inch (four to five cm) deep surface layer of fine granules.

FERTILIZERS

For information about plant foods, see "The Background to Soil Improvement Practices" at the end of this chapter. Fertilizers are used to supply additional foods to plants. There are two classes of fertilizer: organic, derived from animal and vegetable sources, and inorganic or so-called chemical fertilizers. Since plants take up food in inorganic forms, it makes little if any difference whether the foods are derived from organic or inorganic fertilizers. The only advantage to using organic fertilizers is that they generally release nutrients slowly over a longer period, in some cases eventually adding to the humus content of the soil. Disadvantages include low nutrient content in some cases, high unit cost and the release of nutrients too slowly.

Nitrogen(N), phosphorous(P) and potassium(K) are the most common nutrient elements in most fertilizers. By law, the percentage of these foods must be stated on the package. They are expressed as three numbers: for example 10-30-10, means that this fertilizer contains 10 per cent N, 30 per cent P and 10 per cent K. These numbers always represent N-P-K in that order.

Unit analysis compares the cost per unit of a specific food in different fertilizers. The method is to divide the cost of each fertilizer being compared by the percentage of the food it contains, that you wish to compare. As a hypothetical example, let's look at the unit cost of N in three fertilizers. 10-30-10 @ $30 / 100# has a unit cost of $30/10 or $3. The unit cost of 16-20-0 @ $40 is $2.50 and 33-0-0 @ $50 is $1.52. Although the cost per 100# of 33-0-0 is highest, its cost per unit of N is lowest.

APPLICATION

Rates of application vary with the crop and purpose. See specific chapters for detailed information or follow directions on the package.

The most common method of application is broadcasting, spreading the fertilizer on the soil surface. In the cultivation of vegetables, application in or to the side of seed rows is sometimes recommended. Water-soluble kinds may be applied directly to the root zone of plants and in the case of those kinds absorbed through the leaves, directly to the foliage.

To avoid burning foliage during or following application of dry fertilizers
- **apply at the correct rate**
- **spread evenly and uniformly over the soil surface or lawn**
- **unless it's a liquid foliar fertilizer, don't apply to leaves unless immediately followed by watering to wash it off**
- **apply to moist soil**
- **don't apply to wet foliage**
- **do water after application**

COMPOSTING

Well-rotted garden refuse is a valuable source of excellent, low-cost, organic matter. Just about any material of vegetable origin can be used as long as it's not too woody.

Several compact forms of compost container systems are available. Traditional methods are open heaps and side-by-side double or triple containers, usually made of wood.

The production of well-rotted, granular, non-slimy, sweet smelling compost is accomplished by aerobic decomposition, which at minimum requires oxygen, water and the appropriate oxygen breathing bacteria.

Note. **When using a double-bin technique, the compost is turned from bin to bin two or more times depending on the rate of decomposition.**

Some gardeners place a few evenly-spaced, shallow layers of top soil through the heap to inject bacteria and accelerate decomposition.

The introduction of three inch (7.5 cm) deep layers of fresh, strawy stable or barnyard manure every 12-15 inches (30-37.5 cm) will also hasten decomposition and enrich the resulting compost. However, a temporary, unpleasant smell may be a price to be paid.

Shallow, even-depth layers of grass clippings are a useful addition. They are best when allowed to wilt before placing them on the heap. The grass must be cut a minimum of three times after spraying with herbicide before adding it to the compost pile.

The length of time it takes to make good compost in the Vancouver area is about six months.

The fundamental method requires
- a level, well-drained site where surplus water can run away from the bottom of the compost heap
- spreading the different kinds of raw organic matter in even layers of uniform depth
- a maximum heap-height of six feet (1.8 m)
- sprinkling each one foot (30 cm) depth of material with water, and a high nitrogen liquid or dry fertilizer
- after building to full height, allowing the heap to settle approximately one half its height
- starting at one end of the heap, using a fork to turn it over, moving it a couple of feet to the left or right
- during turn-over, loosening any compacted material and water dry spots
- re-shaping and tidying the heap
- allowing the heap to settle, then turn it over and reshape

The compost is now ready for use as a soil amendment or mulch.

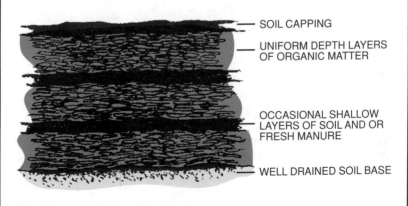

SOIL CAPPING

UNIFORM DEPTH LAYERS OF ORGANIC MATTER

OCCASIONAL SHALLOW LAYERS OF SOIL AND OR FRESH MANURE

WELL DRAINED SOIL BASE

THE BACKGROUND TO SOIL IMPROVEMENT PRACTICES

WHERE PLANTS OBTAIN FOODS

Plants obtain their nutrients from two basic sources: the atmosphere and the soil.

Atmosphere   Carbon dioxide, obtained from the atmosphere, is used in photosynthesis, the process by which chlorophyll-containingplants manufacture simple sugars using energy from sunlight.

Respiration, the reverse of photosynthesis, uses oxygen to burn or break down simple sugars, thereby releasing stored energy derived from the sun, making it available for growth.

Soil water   Hydrogen is obtained from soil water and used in photosynthesis.

The soil   All other plant foods are obtained from the soil, including nitrogen and sulphur, which are essential in the formation of proteins, the building blocks of living organisms. Hence the fundamental importance of soil improvement to increase fertility and make soil-borne nutrients readily available to plants.

ESSENTIAL PLANT FOODS

While about 60 chemical elements have been found in plants, only 16 are generally considered to be essential for healthy growth. They are classified as macro and micro nutrients, based on the amounts used by plants, not on their nutritional importance.

Macro nutrients include, carbon, oxygen and hydrogen (obtained from air and water) and nitrogen, phosphorous, potassium, sulphur, magnesium and calcium (from the soil).

Micro nutrients contained in the soil include chlorine, boron, iron, manganese, zinc, copper and molybdenum. Since very small amounts are required and many naturally-occurring soils contain them in adequate quantities, they are generally available to plants. When specific shortages occur, they may be added to the soil or fed to plants in a suitable chemical form.

The three soil-borne foods of greatest concern to most gardeners and required in the largest amounts are nitrogen, phosphorous and potassium.

Nitrogen is an essential constituent of protein. It helps to produce healthy, lush growth of new shoots and leaves, and promotes a dark green colour.

Phosphorous promotes the development of strong, healthy root systems, the setting of shoot and flower buds and the quality of flowers and seeds.

Potassium is involved in the development of the mechanical strength of stems and roots, and resistance to diseases.

Other macro nutrients required in smaller amounts include sulphur, which promotes rich green colour; calcium, to glue plant cells together; and iron and magnesium, both required in the development of chlorophyll, which makes possible the process of photosynthesis and the production of sugar and starch.

SOIL COMPOSITION

Most soils are made up of five basic components: minerals, organic matter, water, air and soil organisms.

Minerals   In gardener's terms the mineral component comprises clay, silt and sand.

Clay is made up of very tiny (in some cases microscopic), mineral particles. They are flat-shaped and very tightly packed. Due to the huge combined surface area of the particles, they hold a lot of water. While cold, wet and difficult to cultivate, clays contain plenty of plant foods. They also combine with humus, derived from organic matter, forming the chemically active, food producing, clay-humus colloids. (See "Organic Matter," below).

Sand comprises large, rough, uneven, sometimes rounded particles. It is fast draining, holding little water. Manures and other forms of organic matter are quickly used up in sands. Generally, they contain small quantities of plant foods and are not very fertile. However, they are loose structured and easy to work.

Silt particles are larger than clay but smaller than sand. They are intermediate between both in their qualities, which vary with particle size. When fine, they can be wet and sticky, but are well-drained and dry when coarse. Silts are often mixed with fine sands.

A GARDENER'S COMPARISON OF CLAY AND SAND

Here, in gardener's terms, is a common sense comparison of the major characteristics of clay and sand. Silts will fall somewhere between, depending on their particle size.

	CLAY SOILS	SANDY SOILS
Cultivation	*Heavy*	*Light*
Water Content	*Wet*	*Dry*
Temperature	*Cold*	*Warm*
Spring Warm-up	*Late*	*Early*
Food Content	*Rich*	*Poor*
Food Availability	*Unwilling*	*Willing*
Holding Power	*Miserly*	*Spendthrift*

Organic matter   Organic matter is made up of the decomposing remains of plants and animals. By the action of insects, fungi and bacteria in the soil, it is broken down to form humus, a dark brown to blackish, formless substance which is the end product of decomposition. During the process, plant foods are returned to the soil, enriching it and increasing fertility. Carbon dioxide is also produced. It combines with water, forming mild carbonic acid which breaks down minerals, releasing plant foods.

In sandy soils, humus helps bind the loose particles into firmer aggregates and acts as a sponge, retaining water. When mixed with clay, it opens up the soil by separating particles, improving porosity and drainage, and by helping to develop aggregates of soil particles, thereby improving workability. It also takes part in the formation of clay-humus colloids, thereby enhancing the availability of plant foods and fertility.

Soil water   A mixture of water, weak carbonic acid and dissolved plant foods is contained in the spaces between the soil particles. It also forms a film around the particles. Soil water exists in two states: "unavailable" (or tightly bound to the particles and not available to plant roots) and "available" to plant roots. It is "available" water which is of most interest to gardeners and plants.

Soil air   Oxygen, carbon dioxide and other atmospheric gases are contained in the spaces between soil particles. As previously mentioned, oxygen is required by roots for respiration. Carbon dioxide is dissolved in water to form carbonic acid which helps release nutrients from soil minerals. In water-logged soils where oxygen is excluded from the air spaces, asphyxiation of the roots may occur.

Soil organisms   A variety of small mammals, insects, worms, molluscs, protozoa, fungi and bacteria inhabit fertile soils. Through their feeding, digesting and eliminating activities, they break down organic matter, resulting in humus formation and the release of plant foods, thereby enriching the soil. They are essential to the decomposition of organic matter and humus formation.

Fertile soils contain an abundance of micro-organisms which are dependent on adequate organic matter for their survival. There is, therefore, a reciprocal relationship between organic matter, biological activity and fertility.

GARDENING IN SMALL SPACES

This chapter is aimed at the urban gardener who doesn't have an abundance of space.

Small spaces include townhouse, courtyard and balcony gardens.

Plants in such gardens may be grown in smaller versions of the ground level beds and borders used in larger urban gardens. Raised planting areas, planters and various kinds of containers are characteristic features. Gardening on apartment balconies is usually restricted exclusively to growing plants in containers.

Due to space limitations, planning should be carried out with considerable care. For general planning considerations, see Chapter 2, Garden Planning. Special planning requirements will be mentioned as appropriate.

CREATING YEAR ROUND EFFECTS

In Vancouver we can have colour in the garden all year round. Many plants bloom or carry berries even in the winter. Early bulbs like winter aconite and snow drops, Christmas roses, witch hazel, *Viburnum*, jasmine and *Chimonanthus* all flower in the winter. Small trees and shrubs like *Pernettia, Skimmia, Callicarpa*, and *Cornus mas* have wonderful berries. Spring is magnificent with colour from bulbs, camelias, rhododendrons, and azaleas. For summer colour there are annuals, perennials, summer bulbs and shrubs like *Hibiscus, Choisya*, and climbers like *Clematis*. Due to mild temperatures, many summer-flowering plants carry well into the fall to be augmented with fall flowering plants like *Schizostylis, Gentiana* and *Nerine*.

As well as flowers, consider plants with interesting textures, shapes and bark. To create a bigger impact, group plants together rather than stringing them out in a row or scattering them throughout the garden. Three primroses make a statement if grown together, while they may get lost if separated. Take advantage of vertical space. A vine does not need to climb up a trellis — let it climb a tree to increase your enjoyment. The vine might complement the tree's blossoms by blooming at the same time or blooming later to give colour over a longer period.

Grow bulbs and annuals in containers which can be moved about the garden to provide colour and interest where needed. With careful planning, your garden will always have something interesting to catch your eye.

These are distinctive features of small gardens.

PLANTERS

The more or less permanent, fixed planting areas of many small landscapes impart a basic sense of design. Not likely to be found on balconies, they include

- grade level holes of various shapes and sizes, cut into paved and grass areas
- peripheral and other borders at ground level
- raised, wall-retained, planting areas and borders of various shapes and heights
- open-top planter walls
- large containers, too heavy to move frequently

CONTAINERS

Portable boxes, dishes, pots, vases and urns may be planted. They can be made of wood, concrete, baked clay, plastic and ceramic materials. Containers are available in a wide range of designs and materials, from simple clay and terra-cotta flower pots to elaborate Grecian urns made of stone and large concrete boxes.

For growing vegetables, particularly on balconies, small wooden boxes are ideal since they can be moved without heroic measures. When several are carefully arranged and planted, significant production may be achieved.

A wide variety of plants, including small trees, perennials, annuals, vines, and vegetables, can be grown successfully in containers. As long as they drain properly, containers can be made of almost any material.

A practical size is 48 inches (120 cm) long, 16 inches (40 cm) wide and 12 inches (30 cm) deep, the box, sitting on two 2 x 4 inch (5 x 10 cm) runners to keep them off the ground, thereby ensuring adequate drainage and preventing rot. Use three-quarter inch (2 cm) particle board or plywood, treated with a non-petroleum based wood preservative and lined with a 4 mil, polyethylene film.

Window boxes are available in wood, plastic and metal. In addition to gracing windows, they may be used along the sides of railings and fences, on top of fences and screens, and as low planters in a variety of settings.

PLANTS TO GROW IN CONTAINERS

Containers are the only way many people can garden and there is a wide choice of plants to grow this way. The dwarf Alberta spruce tree, fruit trees, peonies, azaleas and smaller rhododendrons will grow well in containers. Try hardy perennials such as *Achillia, Artemisia, Dianthus,* pansies, *Viola odorata,* and *Cyclamen.* Experiment with other perennials. If you grow them from seed, you will only have lost your time if they succumb to the cold. Almost any annual, including vines such as morning glory and sweet peas, will grow in a container. Hardy vines such as *Clematis* and ivy will survive, too. Last, but not least, vegetables will grow in containers. Asparagus, cucumbers, lettuce, squash and even corn, if a half barrel is used, will grow on your deck.

DRAINAGE

It is important to ensure that surplus water can freely drain out of planters and containers. As long as containers have an unobstructed drainage hole in the bottom covered by a wire or plastic mesh screen, broken crocks or coarse gravel, impeded drainage is not likely to be a problem.

If the underlying soil is well drained, open bottom planters should not be a problem. Be sure that solid bottom planters have drainage holes. In large, solid bottom planters, over 24 inches (60 cm) deep, place a four inch (10 cm) layer of coarse gravel in the bottom before filling with soil.

SOILS

For ground level and raised open bottom planters, any well worked, medium loam garden soil will be satisfactory for most plants. See Chapter 3 for soil improvement methods.

For solid bottom planters and containers, use a soil mix comprising by bulk 7 parts, medium - heavy loam, 3 parts, sterilized, granular, fibrous, sphagnum peat moss and 2 parts, coarse, washed, angular particle sand with most particles between 1/16 and 1/8 of an inch (15 and 30 mm) across. Add three ounces (85 g) of lime and six ounces (170 g) of 5-10-5 fertilizer to each 2.5 cubic feet (.7 m^2) of compost. Omit the lime if plants that need acid soil are to be grown.

On balconies, the weight of this compost may be reduced by using perlite or vermiculite instead of sand.

"Cornell type" mix is a popular, light-weight medium suitable for containers. It comprises equal parts of sterilized, granular peatmoss and #4 grade vermiculite. To each 2.5 cubic feet (0.7 m³) of mix, add and mix in thoroughly 10 level tablespoons (150 ml) of ground limestone, 5 level tablespoons (75 ml) of saltpeter and one gallon (4.5 L) of warm water.

When mixing any compost, the peat moss must first be thoroughly moistened. Mix the peat and sand or vermiculite. Add and mix in the water to moisten. Finally mix in the loam and/or fertilizers.

Before filling a container, cover the drainage holes with pieces of 1/8 inch (3 mm) galvanized wire or plastic mesh to prevent the soil mix from running out. When using a heavy soil mix in containers over 10 inches (25 cm) deep, place a one inch (2.5 cm) layer of peat moss or styrofoam balls, pellets or chips over the bottom prior to filling. Fill with soil mix, lightly compacting each four inch (10 cm) layer with the fingers. Leave a 3/4 inch (2 cm) deep watering space between the soil surface and container rim. Using a watering can or hose with a spray head, water thoroughly to settle the soil.

WATERING

Due to the smaller volumes of soil in planters and containers, plus faster drainage as a result of being raised above ground level, watering will generally be needed more frequently than in garden beds, especially in hot dry weather. Serious consideration should be given to the use of trickle irrigation and wick watering systems, especially on balconies.

Containers on balconies are particularly vulnerable, drying out quickly and frequently. The problem is often compounded by a frequently absent gardener.

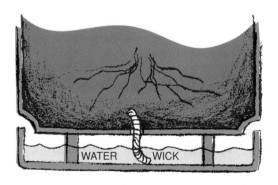

Containers on balconies tend to dry out very quickly, because of the combination of small soil masses, exposed containers, wind, and sun. Wick watering systems are invaluable to the frequently absent or forgetful gardener.

FERTILIZING

As a result of a smaller soil volume and nutrient leaching in small planters and containers, the amount and frequency of fertilizing will be increased, particularly for container grown vegetables, annuals and other bedding plants. Vigorous herbaceous perennials and ground covers in smaller raised planters will need the same careful attention to fertilizing. On the other hand, it may be necessary to reduce the amount of fertilizer for small trees and larger shrubs to restrict their rate of growth.

Dwarf shrubs will require restricted fertilizing.

Trees and shrubs in grade level, open borders should be treated as in any other garden setting, requiring fertilizing once each spring.

MULCHING

In late spring or early summer, a two inch (five cm) deep layer of well rotted manure or compost over the soil surface will help to retain soil water, keep the soil cool, provide a mild feed and suppress annual weeds. When forked into the soil each year in late fall, it will continually replenish its organic matter content.

WINTER PROTECTION

Small containers and narrow window boxes containing permanent plants need winter protection. They may be sunk up to their rim in the garden or in a larger container of soil. Plants in half-barrel sized containers survive our coldest weather without protection. Most winters, 12 x 12 inch (30 x 30 cm) containers are fine. It is a good idea to place containers as close together as possible in a protected area. They will help to protect each other. If a bad freeze is forecast, wood chips, moss, burlap or even crumpled newspaper pushed between the pots will help to insulate them.

If garden space is available it is always a good idea to sink all but the largest containers up to their rims in the soil. If roots are protected, the foliage is not usually damaged. Don't forget hanging baskets once summer is over, since few plants are hardy enough to survive winter in them.

TYPES OF PLANTS

LOCAL SELECTION

Here is a selection of plants suitable for small gardens and garden spaces in the Vancouver region. For more specifics on growing flowers, shrubs and trees, refer to Chapters 5, 7, and 8.

TREES AND SHRUBS

Although an occasional, carefully-located, larger specimen tree or shrub may be permitted in the larger small garden, as a general rule most plants will be of the naturally small and dwarf variety.

> *Rhododendron yakusimanum*, azaleas, Japanese maples, *Pieris japonica, Calluna* species, *Chaenomeles speciosa, Daphne cneorum, Erica* species, *Euonymus fortunei, Cornus mas* (Cornelian Cherry), Mugo Pine, *Acer circinatum* (Vine maple).
>
> Some columnar, pyramidal and fastigiate plants are particularly useful and eye-appealing in small spaces:
> *Juniperus communis 'Compressa', Juniperus virginiana*, the globular or oval *Abies balsamea* 'Nana', *Thuja occidentalis* 'Tiny Tim.'
>
> Slow growers like junipers and dwarf conifers, and those like yew and cedar which are suitable for clipping.
>
> Plants which are suitable for restrictive pruning are also easily adapted to a small garden:
> *Photinia x fraseri, Camelia japonica, Eleagnus angustifolia, Ilex aquifolium* (Holly)

CLIMBERS

Climbing plants are excellent in the small garden. They may be trained to climb up or cascade down walls, fences, screens, pillars, poles, trellises, pergolas and slopes. Climbers can provide delicate vertical tracery or dense screens of foliage, and strong vertical accents, without using much space at ground level. There are many suitable climbers.

> *Clematis alpina, C. montana, C. orientalis, Wisteria,* ivy, *Akebia quinata, Lonicera* (honeysuckle), *Parthenocissus* species

Non-invasive ground covers may be used to link together groups of taller plants and to carpet parts of the garden floor, cover slopes and mounds, create interesting horizontal tapestries and prevent weeds.

> *Arctostaphylos uva-ursi,* 'Vancouver Jade' (bear berry), *Genista pilosa,* 'Vancouver Gold' (dwarf broom), *Microbiota decussata* (Russian cypress), *Cotoneaster horizontalis* , *Hedera helix* (ivy), *Jasminum nudiflorum* (winter blooming jasmine), *Pachysandra* species, *Epimedium* species

Non-climbing shrubs suitable for training against walls, screens and fences are also very useful since they require less space than those allowed to grow naturally out in the open. One plant suitable for training against walls or fences is *Cotoneaster horizontalis.*

FRUIT TREES

Fruit trees may be grown in a small garden if they are grafted on dwarfing rootstocks like the apple M 27 or if they are natural dwarfs such as the Dwarf Stella Cherry. Fruit trees may be espaliered along a wall or fence or on wires strung between posts. By training and pruning from the time they are first grafted they are kept in a two dimensional plane. Small fruit trees may be grown in tubs on patios or decks.

The care, culture, varieties, training and pruning of fruit trees is discussed further in Chapter 7.

HERBACEOUS PERENNIALS

Many perennials are suitable for small gardens and containers. Perennials may be used as accent plants, as a ground cover or as foils to other plants. The foliage and flowers may be of different textures, growth habit and colour, to add interest to the landscape.

Avoid invasive perennials unless they are restricted in isolated beds or grown in containers.

Hostas, primroses, lupins, *Bergenia, Lamium* and the true, hardy geraniums do well in shady sites. In the sun, plant evening primrose, *Dianthus,* many of the smaller herbs — lavender, sage and thyme — and creeping *Phlox.* Do not overlook the ornamental grasses and ferns which add another dimension to the beds.

The care and culture of perennials is discussed in Chapter 5.

BULBS, CORMS AND TUBERS

Bulbs are a natural in small gardens as most of them do not take up much space and may be grown in containers. In Vancouver, the spring bulbs will be showing up from Christmas through to May as the different varieties and cultivars come into bloom.

Some bulbs to grow, starting with the earliest, are *Galanthus* or snowdrops, *Crocus*, the daisy-like *Anemone blanda, Iris reticulata*, and *Muscari*, the grape hyacinth. Tulips follow, with the early species that are small and dainty, including the gregii and fosteriana varieties, then the more stately Darwins and other later tulips. Daffodils come in mid-spring, followed by Dutch iris and *Alliums*. As summer progresses, there are lilies, and in the fall the dainty fall crocus and colourful mauve *Colchicum* appear. These can all be grown in containers, although hyacinths are better planted in the ground, as they are more tender.

PRUNING TREES AND SHRUBS

Bear in mind that a plant's root environment will affect its rate of shoot growth and, therefore, pruning practices. Those planted in open, ground-level beds and borders and larger, open bottom, raised containers will generally produce more shoot growth than plants in solid bottom, raised planters and containers.

In general, pruning practices will be similar to those used in normal size gardens. See Chapter 8, Trees and Shrubs for additional information.

Each year during the dormant period, all trees and shrubs should be checked. Where appropriate, normal form and maintenance pruning should be carried out. Special techniques that apply to small spaces include:

- during the dormant period, that is before any sign of new growth, plants trained against walls, fences and screens should have overcrowded shoots thinned out, long un-branched shoots shortened and very vigorous, unruly shoots completely removed back to their point of origin on major framework branches and trunk(s).
- plants trained against walls and trellises, etc. that flowered on the previous year's shoots should have all flowered shoots cut back to one or two buds beyond their points of origin on the permanent, mature branches which are trained to the wall or fence. This should be carried out immediately after the flowers have faded.
- plants trained against walls or fences that bloom on the current year's shoots should have last year's flowered shoots cut back to one or two buds beyond their point of origin. Carry out this work in late winter or early spring while plants are completely dormant.
- plants kept small by restrictive pruning (including restricted forms of fruit trees) should be subject to normal form and

maintenance pruning. However they may also be pruned in the first week in July by shortening all new side shoots produced from the framework branches during the current year to three or four leaves beyond their point of origin on the framework branches.

GROWING VEGETABLES IN CONTAINERS

The economics of small garden production using containers is not the same as using open soil. Scale is smaller but productivity may be higher. Costs can also be higher since the growing environment must first be constructed. Cost also depends on standards chosen. For example, manufactured containers cost more than do-it-yourself kinds, which in turn cost more than recycled containers, formerly used for other purposes. Here's an example of a home-made container and its uses. It starts with a 3/4 inch (2 cm) particle board box, nailed, glued, painted and lined with 4 mil polyethylene film. It is 48 inches (120 cm) long, 16 inches (40 cm) wide and 12 inches (30 cm) deep, sitting on two 2 x 2 inch (5 x 5 cm) runners. The box holds

- two 16 inch (40 cm) rows of bunching onions, sown at the ends
- 12 station sown leaf or small head lettuce, spaced 8 inches (20 cm) apart and 4 inches (10 cm) in from the sides
- 3 cordon type tomatoes planted 16 inches (40 cm) apart down the middle. Onions and lettuce are sown April 1 and tomatoes planted May 20 if covered with hot caps or June 1 without.

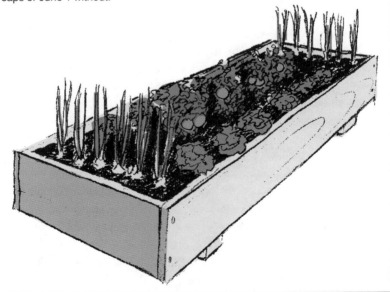

All kinds of vegetables may be successfully grown in containers. Traditional window boxes with inside dimensions of 10 inches (25 cm) wide and 8 inches (20 cm) deep, of any convenient, easily-handled lengths are also suitable for salad and root vegetables as well as annual flowers. Various shaped containers, approximately 12 inches (30 cm) x 12 inches (30 cm) and 10 inches (25 cm) deep, are very useful for single plants of large, space-using kinds, including cucumber, tomato, zucchini, eggplant and pepper.

Apart from the previously discussed problems associated with watering, water conservation and fertilizing, all other cultural practices are similar to those discussed in Chapter 6.

ARCHITECTURAL FEATURES

Walls, fences, screens, trellises, pergolas, arches, pillars, statuary, sculpture, stone work, pools and fountains are particularly appropriate in smaller gardens. All form strong, permanent vertical accents, providing high visual appeal and interest without using much space at ground level.

See Chapter 2, Garden Planning, for additional information.

BALCONIES

There are a few inherent restrictions in the development of balcony gardens:

- consider access: lumber, boxes, soil and plants must be carried up and down stairwells, in elevators and through patio doors and windows
- weight is an important factor: a balcony must be able to support containers, soil and water, plus the gardener and friends
- generally, the safest place for the heaviest items is next to the building walls, but check with the building owner to be sure
- if in doubt about the structural strength of a balcony, have it checked by an engineer
- water will be needed and an outdoor faucet is ideal. However, light weight plastic hoses can easily be attached to the kitchen faucet. Trickle irrigation and wick watering are particularly appropriate.
- drainage is a related problem: ensure that drainage water follows the balcony's built-in path for shedding rainwater to minimize drip problems for people below
- ensure that items can't roll or be blown off the balcony, endangering people below

- protect building walls and balcony floors, particularly if made of wood, from contact with soil and water. Place a 4-6 mil sheet of polyethylene between soil and building surfaces
- place the bases of containers on bricks or blocks, raising them above the floor to ensure good drainage and prevent rot
- consider scale and don't use all available space for gardening.
- plan carefully, leaving enough space for working, entertaining and sitting out

THE MICRO CLIMATE

Gardening in the air presents the challenge of a new environment. The closer a balcony is to the sun, the higher the light intensity. Unfortunately, higher light potential is often modified. Balconies may be shaded by adjacent buildings, trees, enclosures and other balconies. Aspect is also important. South and south west facing balconies receive the most direct light. East facing balconies get sun from early morning until approximately noon and west facing from noon until evening. Except in early morning and late evening during summer, north facing locations receive little direct sun but, when unobstructed, are reasonably light on bright days. Most balconies tend to be shadier next to the building wall than at the railings.

Although there are structural and climatic limitations on balcony gardening, with a little careful planning you can add colour and life to almost any space.

Since many variables affect direct sunlight and light intensity, the best course is to observe the degree of light penetration and patterns on the balcony. Make an inventory of sunny and shady spots, noting duration and time of day and year. Determine where light intensity can be increased by reflection. Paint walls white, install reflector boards and mirrors. Replace solid enclosures with open railings, clear plastic or heavy glass. If practical, remove nearby trees. To be really sophisticated, install supplemental artificial lighting.

On warm, sunny balconies it may be necessary to provide for cooling shade. Blinds, curtains, screens and trellises may be used.

Wind is a special problem, particularly on the upper balconies of high-rise apartments. Often it's a case of the higher the balcony the stronger the wind. Provide protection by using trellises, baffles and screens. Some enthusiasts use clear plastic or heavy glass. Secure taller plants by tying them to walls, railings, trellises, nets, poles and stakes.

A major problem results from the combination of small soil masses, exposed containers, wind and sun. Soils in containers dry out very quickly — a problem often compounded by a frequently absent gardener. On a balcony, watering delayed may be the equivalent of watering denied. Quick justice in the form of early crop demise may result. Trickle irrigation and wick watering systems should be considered.

USE OF VERTICAL SPACE

Using strong brackets, clamps and other fasteners, smaller flower boxes may be attached to railings and walls. Depending on available light and vertical space, they may be arranged in more than one level. Unless special drainage arrangements are made, hang flower boxes and baskets inside the railings — not over the street. Arrange containers at various heights by placing them on bricks, blocks, benches and tables, etc. Containers placed on boards with castors can be moved against a wall for protection from wind, hail and frost, to follow the sun or be moved indoors when fall frosts hit, thereby extending the growing season.

Air space may be used to good effect. Hanging pots and baskets may be attached to the underside of the balcony above, on pole hangers and wall brackets. Be sure to use only heavy duty brackets, fasteners, chains, wire and ropes.

CHAPTER 5

FLOWER GARDENING

TYPES OF FLOWERS

Flowers are divided into groups according to their life cycles — perennial, biennial, annual — and whether they are bulbous, hardy or tender.

HERBACEOUS

Herbaceous plants develop non-permanent, non-woody shoots that die back to ground level at the end of each growing season. There are three classes.

Perennials live for three or more growing seasons. They over-winter as dormant, underground or near ground level bulbs, corms, tubers, tuberous roots, and dormant roots or dormant shootlet systems from which new shoots, foliage and flowers are produced each growing season. From a cultural point of view, there are two basic kinds:

> Hardy, which includes all herbaceous, over-wintering garden plants, usually called perennials, such as *Delphinium*, lupin, lily, *Hosta*, *Peony* and *Astilbe*.
> Tender, which won't reliably survive the winter outdoors, including the old favourites, *Dahlia*, *Gladiolus*, and tuberous *Begonia*.

Biennials live two growing seasons. During the first, they grow from seed, forming a non-flowering rosette of foliage which over-winters. In the next growing season, they elongate, flower, set seed and die. Canterbury bell, forget-me-nots, sweet William and foxglove are biennial.

Annuals like petunias, marigolds and *Lobelia* live one growing season, during which they grow from seed, flower, set seed and die. In addition to the true annuals, some are tender perennials. Geraniums, snapdragons, marguerites, and *Fuchsia* are treated as annuals since they flower from seed in one season, although technically, they are tender woody perennials. In Vancouver, snapdragons and geraniums will survive outside, some winters, in a protected corner.

USES

In Chapter 2, Garden Planning, different ways were discussed for using herbaceous plants in the landscape, including herbaceous borders, mixed plantings, combined with annuals and shrubs or as ground covers. Herbaceous plants do not have to be restricted to a flower garden. If space is at a premium, grow some in the vegetable garden. Many annuals and perennials do well in containers and hanging baskets. Bedding plants can be used to create a formal garden or to give the garden a more casual feeling.

Shrubs and trees give the garden form, but herbaceous plants complete the picture. Choose herbaceous plants with contrasting textures, shapes and colours to complement each other. Look for plants that not only look good in flower but have interesting foliage throughout the season. The leaves may have an unusual texture, colour or shape. Try planting a purple-leafed smoke bush, *Cotinus coggygria*, with some pink alliums and the low growing pink *Oenothera speciosa* for an interesting combination. Don't be afraid to move plants around and try different combinations until you find a combination that pleases you. Watch for colour echoes; for example, a flower with a pale green throat which matches the leaf colour of another plant. Grown together, these plants are stunning.

Plant breeding has not only produced new cultivars with large flowers and a wide range of colours but compact plants that flower over long periods of time. Disease and pest resistance and hardiness are also important results of plant breeding programs.

PURCHASING PLANTS - WHAT TO LOOK FOR

BARE ROOT PLANTS

When buying bare root plants, available only in early spring, look for those that are still dormant, without large, green shoots. Roots should not be dried out or broken. Tuberous roots should be plump. Dahlias, irises, bleeding hearts and peonies are often available bare rooted.

Check carefully to be sure that the roots of bare root plants are not broken or dried out.

CONTAINER GROWN PLANTS

Container grown perennials and biennials are available throughout spring and summer, but for the best selection, shop in the spring.

Perennials may be grown from seed, cuttings or divisions. They are sold mainly in four inch (10 cm) pots or one gallon (4.5 L) containers. Seed-grown perennials such as pansy, *Dianthus*, and *Coreopsis* are often available like bedding plants — four to a container.

If you are looking for unusual perennials, shop at spring plant sales by garden societies and botanical gardens. The "Shop In The Garden" at the University of British Columbia has unusual plants for sale most of the year.

BEDDING PLANTS

When buying bedding plants, annuals and some perennials, look for healthy, compact plants. Leaf colour should be mid to dark green with no yellowing. Plants should not be leggy (the stems should not have elongated to reach the light), and there should not be masses of roots coming out of the drainage holes. You can check the roots by holding the plant upside down and lightly tapping the rim of the container on the corner of a bench or table. The root ball will slip out of the pot. The roots will be visible and should cover two thirds of the soil. If the soil is a mass of roots, the plant has been in that container too long and should have been potted-on into a larger pot. The plant will be stressed and may not perform well in the garden. Look around the garden centre. Is it clean, with well watered plants and no sign of wilted, sick-looking plants? The health of the plants you are buying will be a reflection of how the garden centre looks. Most annuals should have their tips pinched-back to encourage branching. This sometimes means you will be removing flower buds, but despite the slight set back you will have a much better flower display throughout the summer.

All plants should be labeled for easy identification.

Bedding plants should appear healthy and compact, with mid to dark green leaf colour, and the soil should not be a mass of roots.

SOIL

Soil preparation is discussed in Chapter 3. Remember to prepare the soil well as some perennials may be in the same spot for many years. When a perennial bed is prepared, remove all weeds, particularly perennial kinds, and dig in a two inch (five cm) deep layer of organic matter, compost, sea weed or well rotted manure. Prepare the bed several weeks before the plants are set out. This will give annual weeds a chance to grow. Shuffle a hoe through the bed, removing the tiny weed seedlings. Do not disturb the soil any deeper than necessary to avoid bringing up more weed seeds to the surface where they can germinate. Many perennials benefit from a two to three inch (five to eight cm deep mulch of organic matter after planting. In the spring, feed them a basic fertilizer like 6-8-6, sprinkled on the soil around the plant but not touching the stems or foliage.

PLANTING

In Vancouver, container-grown perennials may be planted at almost any time, but they are usually available in the spring or fall.

Once the soil has been prepared, dig the hole and position the plant. Match the soil level around the root ball or container with the level of the surrounding soil. It is important not to plant too deeply. Press the soil firmly around the newly planted plant and water. If the day is sunny, prop up a board or something to give it some shade for a day or two, particularly if it is a seedling which doesn't have a root system as mature as that of a plant division. Provide enough space for the plant to grow. Take into consideration its final height and the conditions under which it grows best — sun or shade, dry or moist.

THINNING / PINCHING

Thinning Out   Thinning out is the practice of removing surplus young shoots from the crown of a plant to stimulate remaining shoots to grow taller, stronger and healthier, and to produce larger flowers. Carefully remove the surplus shoots when three inches (7.5 cm) high.

Most kinds of herbaceous perennials that benefit from thinning are those which have one or more of the following characteristics:
- **forming large clumps of vigorous, closely spaced, sometimes invasive, shoots**
- **producing several closely spaced competing shoots originating within a small area**
- **producing a large number of weak, spindly shoots**

There is no need to thin out plants that produce a few, non-competing shoots from a small, definite, slow growing crown.

Timing   Thinning out should be carried out early in the growing season, before new shoots are more than three inches (7.5 cm) long. Staking should be done at the same time.

Pinching Out   Pinching out tip-growth with the thumb and forefinger will cause the plant to send out side shoots, and the plant will become bushy and more compact. It will flower later but have more blooms. Chrysanthemums and asters are good candidates for pinching. In May or June, remove the top three inches (7.5 cm) of growth back to just above a leaf. Chrysanthemums are usually pinched once more a month later.

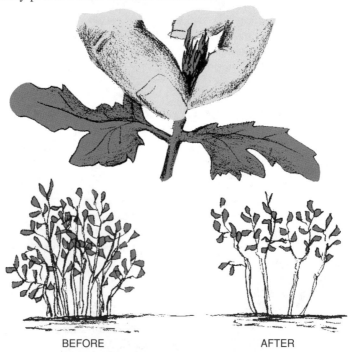

BEFORE   AFTER

Pinching out (removing tip growth from shoots) helps a plant become more bushy and produce more flowers. Thinning out (removing surplus shoots) stimulates remaining shoots to grow taller and produce larger flowers.

DIVIDING AND REPLANTING

Division of plants is done when the leaves are dying back in late October through November or in the spring, as early as mid February or March, just as the new growth is starting to show. Plants like peonies have been known to grow in the same spot for a hundred years while lilies and hostas grow well, undivided, for ten or so years. However, many perennials benefit from division every three to five years. Plants that are slow to grow or naturally small may never have to be divided.

If a clump seems to be crowded with many small shoots and the growth is not vigorous, with smaller or fewer flowers, it is time to divide. Some plants send out plantlets from underground roots or shoots, beyond the clump. These may be dug up and replanted elsewhere.

Dig up the plant to be divided. With a sharp knife, cut through the clump and root ball. Some plants, like primroses, which have multiple crowns, will pull apart easily into separate plants and not need to be cut. If the roots are fibrous, or easily recognizable, separate plantlets are attached to the clump, it is easy to divide up the plant.

Divisions of plants like rhizomatous iris, which have swollen root-like stems that spread along the ground, need to have a growing point where the leaves originate. Discard the older rhizomes from the centre of the clump, keeping the outer, newer growth. This perennial is divided in the summer, about two weeks after blooming. Set the divided rhizomes horizontally just at the soil surface. The light brown rhizome needs to be exposed to the sun.

Plants like hostas may be divided without disturbing the parent plant. Take a sharp shovel and remove a clump of the plant from the side either after it has died back in the fall or before the new leaves have unfurled in the spring. Back-fill the resulting hole.

A clump may supply many divisions. Pick the best looking ones and replant them immediately so the roots do not dry out. If this is impossible, heel them in by temporarily covering their roots in another spot such as the vegetable garden. Don't forget to water newly planted divisions!

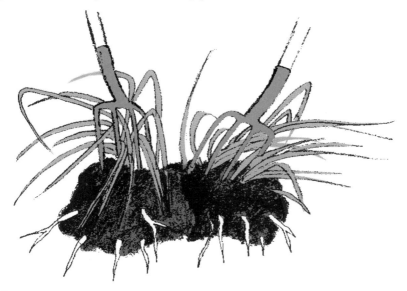

When you divide them, some plants pull apart easily into separate plants and do not need to be cut. Choose the best looking divisions and replant them immediately so that the roots do not dry out.

PERENNIALS FROM SEED

Many perennials are easily grown from seed. If the seeds are collected over the summer they may be sown sparingly in four inch (10 cm) pots in late October. Use a mix of one third soil, one third sand and one third peat. Cover the seeds with a thin layer of soil mix. Top up the pots with small, rounded gravel. Gravel sold for fish tanks is excellent. The gravel slows down the formation of moss and algae, prevents rain damage to the soil, and keeps the emerging stem dryer, helping to prevent disease.

The pots may be left in a sheltered spot in the garden. Under the eaves is fine, but remember they need water and mulch. A cold frame or a cool greenhouse is an excellent place to put pots. Pots may be covered with clear plastic supported on stakes so it does not rest on the emerging seedlings. The seeds will start to germinate from December through to March.

Perennials can be started from seed indoors in the spring. If many seeds are to be sown, a cable that heats soil is a good investment. The top of the refrigerator is usually warm enough. Even a heating pad can be used to supply warmth until the seeds germinate. Once the seeds have germinated, remove them to a sunny window sill or place them under artificial lights. When the seedlings have their first true leaves, the second set to emerge, pot them into individual pots or flats. Harden the seedlings off before they are transplanted outside in late May.

STEM OR ROOT CUTTINGS

Stem cuttings may be taken throughout the growing season. Cuttings of tender perennials are usually taken from mid-August until early September. If plants were over-wintered in a greenhouse or frame, cuttings can be taken

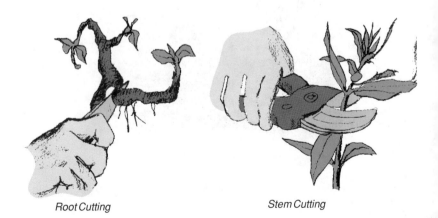

Root Cutting   *Stem Cutting*

in February and March. Using a sharp, clean knife, take a four inch (10 cm) length of stem from the tip of a shoot. Remove the bottom few leaves and any buds or flowers. Insert several cuttings in a four inch (10 cm) pot filled with half perlite and half peat mix. Cover the cuttings with a clear plastic bag to create a moist atmosphere. Cuttings will form roots faster if the soil is warm. If you have soil heating cables, use them. Once the roots have formed, pot the plants individually in regular potting mix, one third peat, one third perlite or sand   and one third potting soil. Over-winter the plants in a cold frame or keep them on the window sill to be planted out in the garden next spring.

STAKING

Many newer cultivars are advertised as non-staking because they have been bred with shorter stems. Unfortunately (depending on how you look at it) in Vancouver perennials grow very well and are often taller than the norm. Tall plants usually need to be staked. Insert several stakes into the ground when the plants start to grow in the spring. String is tied between the stakes and criss-crossed through the middle, forming a network, so the plants will grow up through the spaces. Do not wait until the plant is fully grown and then bunch the whole plant to a single stake. Smaller plants that tend to flop, such as *Dianthus*, can be supported by letting them grow up through small, twiggy branches placed in the soil early in the spring. Mass plantings may be staked by placing stakes in a grid pattern and running twine from stake to stake. The plants will grow up through the grid. This works very well for upright plants like *Gladiolus*. When plants are tied, do it carefully and not too tightly. Ensure that the string does not rub against the stems.

PESTS AND DISEASES

Chapter 10 provides more details on pests and diseases. Perennials are fairly disease and pest free if good gardening practices are maintained. Remove infected plants or leaves when noticed. Do not crowd plants, and do not wet the foliage late in the day or over-fertilize the plants, which leads to soft, weak foliage. Control insects quickly, before their numbers build up. Clean up debris in the fall.

There are a few problems that are pertinent to different species. Sometimes the narcissus bulb fly is a problem, but unfortunately there is no satisfactory cure. The larva invades the bulb to dine and overwinter. Smaller bulbs are killed outright, but larger bulbs may survive over the next few years. Until the bulb recovers, only leaves will grow. Occasionally, peonies may succumb to *Botrytis*, which causes the buds to blacken and dry up. Remove the old foliage in the fall and destroy it. Generally, though, perennials are problem free. The secret is to keep a close watch over the plants, and when the first sign of insect or disease is noticed, correct it before it becomes a problem.

FALL/WINTER CARE

By late October and early November, many of the perennials have died back and the dead leaves may be pulled away and composted. At this time mulch the perennials for winter. A good layer of leaves or compost mulch, four inches (10 cm) thick, helps to protect the plants from cold weather and keeps the soil temperature from fluctuating. The mulch should cover the crown, or in the case of plants that don't die right back to the ground, mulch the soil around the plants. By keeping the soil cool, plants don't start to grow prematurely during the warm spells in the winter. Vancouver can have mild spells during the winter, when we are sure spring has arrived, but they are frequently followed by another cold snap.

If a plant is not reliably winter hardy, take a piece of chicken wire and form an open-ended cage. Weave at least three stakes through the holes in the chicken wire and then push them into the soil to anchor the cage around the plant. Fill the cage with leaves. Once the weather has warmed up in March, remove the cage and compost the leaves.

Take cuttings from tender perennials. They can also be lifted -- carefully dug out of the ground with the roots intact -- and protected in a cold frame, or unheated or very cool greenhouse. Begonias, *Gladiolus*, dahlias and tender bulbs should be lifted and stored in a frost free, cool, dry place.

Tender, woody plants like *Fuchsia* and geraniums can be buried in an 18 inch (45 cm) trench in a well drained spot in the garden for the winter. Under the eaves of the house is a good place. Dig up the plants at the end of February. Cut them back and repot in fresh soil. Set them in a sunny window and they will be ready to plant out in June.

An alternative way to overwinter dormant tender plants is to place the containers in a cardboard box or foam picnic cooler and stuff crumpled newspaper around the pots for insulation. Place the carton in a crawlspace or garage.

Plants which are not winter hardy can be protected in an open ended cage filled with leaves.

Bulb   A bulb is a compressed, telescoped shoot, that has a flattish plate at the base and is usually more or less rounded or pear shaped. The fleshy leaves are folded over each other. On tunicated bulbs, such as tulips and onions, the leaves wrap around the bulb and the outer leaves are thin and papery. Scaly bulbs have leaves that simply overlap each other, as with lilies and fritillarias, and the flowering shoot develops inside the bulb.

Corm   A corm is a compressed, thickened stem, enclosed by thin, papery leaves. The leaves and flower stems arise from buds at the top of the corm and roots from the base. During the growing season, the corm gradually flattens and shrivels. A new corm develops on top of the old corm at the base of the stem. *Gladiolus* and *Crocus* are both corms.

Tuberous Root System   A tuberous root system has thickened, sausage-like, fleshy roots that are attached to the base of the vegetative or flowering shoot. At the end of the season the old shoots die back to ground level. The next season's growth arises from buds at the base of those shoots, not directly from the roots. Dahlias are an example of a tuberous root. During the growing season the tuberous roots increase in number and size. When they are divided, each division must include a piece of the old stem which includes the bud and an attached tuberous root. A piece of the root without a bud will not grow.

Tuber   A tuber is a compressed, thickened stem without any obvious leaves. The shape may vary from the flattened, slightly dished, round form of tuberous begonias to the formless multi-lobed *Anemone* tuber. Vegetative and flowering shoots arise from buds on top of the tuber and roots from the base. The tuber will increase in size during the growing season.

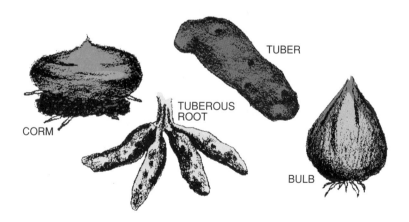

CORM · TUBEROUS ROOT · TUBER · BULB

BULB - CULTIVATION

Tender bulbs, such as tuberous begonias and freesias, must be brought in during the dormant season to a dry, frost free place. Gladiolas and dahlias are semi-hardy and will survive mild winters in Vancouver, if planted in a protected spot. To be on the safe side, however, they should be lifted in the fall after they have been cut back by frost.

Dahlias and gladiolas are cut back to within four inches (10 cm) of the tuber or corm. Leave them to dry on newspaper, then shake off the soil. Dahlias can be divided in the fall or spring. Leave a solid piece of old stem carrying at least one bud per division because new growing points form at the base of the stem. Gladiolas form a new corm each summer. The old shriveled corm and dried leaves will come away, leaving the new corm ready for planting in the spring. Store the bulbs or tubers in peat moss, in a cold, frost free place. Check them during the winter for disease and dehydration. Never store damaged tubers, corms or bulbs.

Hardy bulbs do very well in Vancouver. Although we tend to associate bulbs with spring, there are hardy summer and fall bulbs, too. Starting in January, if the winter is mild, we can enjoy early *Crocus, Scilla, Cyclamen,* snow-drops, winter aconite, *Anemone, Chionodoxa* and reticulata irises. As the weather warms we can have a succession of anemone, daffodils, tulips, hyacinth, *Fritillaria, Erythronium* and *Camassia.* Within each genus — *Narcissus, Tulipa* and *Iris* — there are different species or cultivars that bloom in succession until June. The dainty species *Narcissus* and tulips bloom earlier than the showier cultivars. During the summer, alliums, lilies and hardy *Agapanthus* bloom. In the fall, *Colchicum* or fall crocus sends up its naked stems but that is not the only fall bulb that we can enjoy. Try planting *Crinum, Sternbergia, Crocrosmia, Nerine, Cyclamen* and anemones for late summer and fall colour.

Location and placement of bulbs is discussed in Chapter 2, Garden Planning. Remember, our winters are wet and bulbs need well drained soil. If this is a problem, plant them in raised beds. Dig the soil deeply and incorporate bone meal or a fertilizer that is high in phosphorus and potassium. Fall-blooming bulbs do well when planted under an overhang to protect tender petals from rain. Bulbs should be planted informally in groups rather than marching single file across the flower bed.

Spring-blooming bulbs are planted in October through mid November. Plant bulbs so there is a space of 2 1/2 to 3 times their width between bulbs. Tiny bulbs such as anemones, crocus, eranthis, galanthus, species tulips and narcissus are planted so they are covered with three inches (7.5 cm) of soil. Larger bulbs such as *Fritillaria imperialis,* daffodils and tulips are covered with six inches (15 cm) of soil.

LANDSCAPING

A mixed perennial and rose border.

• Perennials have been successfully interplanted in a large rose collection, grown against a backdrop of tall native trees and ornamental shrubs.

A stepped raised bed makes a colourful entrance along the driveway.

• Raised beds make good sense in our rainy climate because they will drain quickly and warm up fast in the spring.

• A backyard with colourful flower beds, a patio edged with container plants and a lawn. All these elements combine to make the back garden a very usable space for relaxing, entertaining or as a place for children to play.

A brick planter full of colourful perennials and annuals.

Kiwi vines are heavy and must be grown on sturdy supports.

• Small fruits do well in the Vancouver climate, and many gardens contain blueberries, raspberries and strawberries. More and more you will find kiwis. They lend an exotic look to the landscape with their lush growth and fuzzy fruits. Although hardy here, they can be damaged when we have a bad winter.

• Even a small urban lot can contain many different garden areas. This tiny woodland garden is tucked under a tree with a small artificial pond to set the mood. A truly enchanting place.

• Perennial borders must be planned carefully to supply blooms over a long period. Care must be taken to have the colours harmonize, and the ultimate height of each plant must be considered. Perennials tend to grow taller here than the seed packages or reference books suggest.

An artificial pond which looks very natural as the plants tumble over the edges.

U.B.C. Botanical Gardens perennial bed.

TENDER BULBOUS PLANTS

Large-flowered, Pom-pom Dahlia in a container.

• While not the traditional way of growing them, many of the larger-flowered, taller varieties of *Dahlia* are quite at home when grown in 30-40 cm containers. (*left*)

• In this mode, they provide the welcome element of height where several containers are placed together. Additionally, since they are portable, they provide the creative gardener with opportunities to rearrange the landscape from time to time.

• Bear in mind that dahlias in pots, when well-established, require copious watering, especially during hot, dry periods.

Cosmos atrosanguineus — tender, tuberous-rooted perennial.

• Use various kinds of tender bulbous plants to supplement and add variety to annuals and other bedding plants.

• *Dahlias* and *Gladiolus* can provide welcome extra colour in late summer and early fall.

• Long-season, summer-flowering, low carpets of brilliant colour can be created with Multiflora Begonia varieties such as Flamboyant, Helen Harmes and Richard Galle.

Double-flowered, Tuberous Begonia Hybrid (Begonia x tuberhybrida).

Begonia — multiflora hybrids.

• The large-flowering, tuberous begonias grow best in locations exposed to the morning sun, but shaded during the sunniest and warmest part of the day.

• The stiff, upright, sword shaped leaves of *Gladiolus* provide a strong contrast to most hardy perennials.

• Double flowered, hybrid Tuberous Begonias are excellent in 10-15 cm diameter pots and containers. Also try a few large-flowered dahlias in large pots. The tender, tuberous-rooted, perennial, Bloody Cosmos can also be treated as a tender annual. Raise it from seed, in a warm environment, early in the year, just like bedding dahlias. *(above and right)*

Double-flowered, tuberous Begonia Hybrid (Begonia tuberhybrida).

HARDY BULBS

Upward facing Lily Hybrids and Bee Balm (Monarda didyma "Cambridge Scarlet").

• True lilies (*Lilium* species and varieties) are true queens among herbaceous perennials. They are available in a wide range of species, varieties and hybrids. The majority are easy to grow.

• By careful selection, it is possible to have lilies in flower in the garden from May to October.

Puschkinia scilloides — a dwarf, Spring Bulb.

• Many hardy bulbs flower early in the spring, long before most other plants begin their growth cycle. As a consequence, they are an important source of early colour.

• Be generous in your plantings. Most of the smaller bulbs look best when in groups of two to three dozen plants.

• Plant hardy bulbs in early fall, as soon as the bulbs are available in garden centres and department stores.

• Tulips are the most popular bulb flower. They are available in a wide range of kinds from dwarfs such as *Tulipa tarda* to the giant Darwins and *Fosteriana* varieties.

• Bear in mind that planting location will influence the flowering time of tulips. Bulbs in warm, south or southwest facing locations will flower up to six weeks earlier than the same variety in a semi-shaded, cooler place.

• Many dwarf kinds are well suited to sunny spots in the rock garden.

Crocus susianus — an early spring-flowering bulbous plant.

Autumn Crocus (Colchicum autumnale) — a fall-flowering bulb.

Amaryllis belladonna needs a warm spot in the garden.

• Autumn Crocus provides a welcome touch of bright colour prior to the onset of winter.

• There are several species and varieties of Autumn Crocus or *Colchicum*. Most kinds produce their spectacular, crocus-like flowers in the autumn, before the foliage emerges, in stark, colourful contrast with surrounding bare soil.

• The foliage pokes through the soil in the following spring, dying down again in summer.

• Bulbs do very well in Vancouver as long as they are planted in well drained soil and in the sun. Many spring, summer and fall bulbs are enjoyed with most returning year after year to enhance the garden.

ANNUALS

Love-lies-bleeding (Amananthus caudatus) — a tender annual.

• Excepting shrubs and trees with brightly coloured foliage, annuals provide the longest period of summer colour — from June to October, depending on the final fall frost. No other group of herbaceous plants can compete in this arena.

Tree Mallow (Lavetera trimestris) — an annual.

Painted Tongue (Salpiglossis sinuata) — an annual.

• Don't forget that there are many hardy and half-hardy annuals that can be raised from seeds sown directly outside in the garden from mid April to mid May. The keys are sowing thinly and thinning out the resulting seedlings 15-30 cm apart depending on the height and spread of the particular plant.

• When purchasing annual bedding plants, select those that are not crowded in their flats, and short jointed — not long and lank, mid to deep green — not pale green or yellowish. There is no particular merit to plants being in flower, as long as they are of reasonable size.

Moss Rose — (Portulaca grandiflora cultivar).

Castor Bean (Ricinus communis "Impala") — young fruits and male flowers.

• For a truly sub-tropical effect, try Castor Bean Plant and the large-flowered *Datura meteloides*. Use greenhouse-raised, potted seedlings. (*above*)

CONTAINERS & TRELLISES

*Hanging Basket — Ivy-leafed Pelargoniums (Common Geranium),
petunias and the trailing Black-eyed Susan.*

• Most annual flowers are very much at home in containers.

• Drought tolerant kinds such as Pelargoniums, (Common and Ivy-leaved
Geraniums, Petunias, Zinnias, African and French Marigolds, African Daisies
and Dusty Miller are particularly well adapted.

*Hanging container on high trellis — Zonal and Ivy-leaved
Pelargoniums (Common Geraniums) and purple, trailing Lobelia
(Lobelia erinus cultivar).*

• Called the "queen" of climbing plants by many experienced gardeners, Jackman's Clematis and the related members of the Jackman group, deserve a place in every garden. *(left)*

• Keys to success in growing *Clematis* include a shaded root zone, head in the sun and plenty of water and fertilizer during the growing season.

Jackmans Clematis (Clematis x jackmanii) — a summer-flowering climber.

A white, small-flowered Clematis.

• Regular watering is a key to success, especially when the containers are full of well-ramified plant roots and the plants are approaching their peak of development. Check twice daily and water as soon as the soil surface begins to dry and turn lighter coloured. In hot dry weather, one or two waterings per day may be necessary.

Half-round, hanging baskets on an archway wall.

• Place hanging baskets against a background of foliage, stained siding or masonry. Avoid locations where other growing plants can obstruct them from view.

• In hanging baskets, consider both upright-bushy and trailing plants to provide contrast in forms.

• Low, brick-walled planters are excellent when planted with a single, strong coloured bedding plant such as dwarf impatiens and Multiflora Begonias.

An urban back garden — Arcadia Juniper, Marigold, Trellis with hanging baskets, Plastic pots of annuals, and Sumac in the background.

Wisley Gardens (R.H.S.) A demonstration garden with rustic trellis-work, and a raised bed of Red Impatiens.

Containers with Pelargoniums (Geraniums), snapdragons and marigolds.

• Close and open-work trellises are excellent architectural elements in the garden. They may be used to create screens, lath-houses, pillars, pergolas and archways.

Bulbs may be planted by using a bulb planter which makes a hole big enough for one bulb. I prefer to dig a hole big enough for each grouping. I amend the soil, and dig out the hole to the correct depth and level the bottom. Then I space the bulbs in a random pattern, and cover them with soil. Plant each species or cultivar together in a group. Large numbers of bulbs can be planted using a large auger bit on an electric drill. A bulb is dropped in each hole. This method could be used for naturalizing bulbs -- planting them in an area where they can be left undisturbed, such as a woodland garden, grass, or a meadow. The bulbs will multiply over the years, making a lovely show when they bloom.

Small bulbs can be tucked in tiny pockets in a rock garden, or in any other suitable area. The ultimate height and the time of blooming should be considered. Early flowering bulbs are short compared to the later blooming cultivars of *Narcissus* and tulips. Place early blooming plants where they will be enjoyed. Remember that the garden soil will be wet in late winter, so plant them where you have easy access. The very earliest bulbs could be planted near the front door or where they can be enjoyed from a window.

On the coast, bulbs will only need to be watered later in the spring, usually after the bulbs have bloomed and until the foliage dies back. Care should be taken when weeding around bulbs not to damage the bulb. Weeds must be kept removed so they don't compete with the bulbs. Generally, the bulbs are not mulched. Container grown bulbs will need winter protection only if the containers are small. Bulbs in 18 inch (45 cm) clay pots are fine unprotected.

Generally, bulbs are not staked but the tall, later cultivars of tulips have brittle stems and should be planted away from strong winds.

Once the bulbs have bloomed, the spent flower should be nipped off, leaving the stem. The stems and leaves are needed to nourish the bulb. By the time the foliage dies back, the embryo of next year's flower will already have formed. Bulbs do not need to be dug up each year. They may be left and interplanted with annuals.

Early flowering bulbs can be planted under deciduous shrubs or trees where they will bloom before the shrubs or trees leaf out. They can be dug up after they have

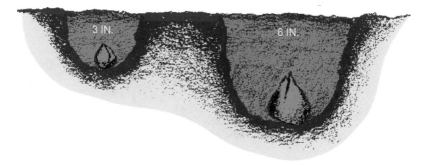

Tiny bulbs, such as anemones and narcissuses, are covered with three inches of soil. Larger bulbs like daffodils and tulips should be covered with six inches of soil. Bulbs should be planted informally in groups rather than marching single file across the flower bed.

died back. Treat them with care because they can be damaged easily, leaving a site for infection. Let them dry off and remove the tiny new bulbs, the most common and easiest way to propagate them. The small bulbs could be planted in a nursery bed for several years until they are large enough to bloom. Label and store bulbs in nylon stockings, onion bags or flat trays, in a cool, airy place until fall when they are replanted. Discard any damaged or diseased bulbs.

Bulbs that are naturalized are left in the ground from year to year and fed 4-10-10 fertilizer in the spring or bone meal in the fall.

Bulbs can be lifted before the foliage dies back by lifting them without disturbing the roots, taking as much soil as possible, and heeling them into the vegetable garden or other out of the way place. Leave the plants until the foliage dies back and then store them until fall. An easier way to lift the bulbs is to plant them in bulb baskets or flower pots which can be lifted with roots intact and transferred to another site. Bulb baskets are mesh baskets filled with soil. The bulbs are planted in them and sunk into the ground. They are often used to prevent rodents from consuming your precious bulbs.

When you are planning a bulb display using a selection of cultivars or different kinds of bulbs, it must be done with care because of the different blooming times, heights and colours of the flowers. For instance, different hyacinth cultivars may bloom at slightly different times, so the display may not turn out as you envisioned. It is safest to plan the display so that if the bulbs do not bloom at the same time it will still look nice. Try planting different cultivars and colours in blocks rather than interspersing them. However, a planting of tulips and daffodils of similar heights, interspersed and blooming at the same time, can be very attractive.

Bulbs can also be interplanted so that the blooms come along in succession. You might start with early *Crocus*, followed by early tulips, daffodils and late tulips. Early blooming bulbs are shorter than later ones. The later blooming bulbs will help to disguise the foliage on the bulbs that have finished blooming.

Bulbs are often planted in mesh baskets to protect them from rodents, and to make it easier to lift them and move them to another site.

Taller bulbs can be under-planted with forget-me-nots and *Cheirianthus* — the wallflower.

To make certain that the plants bloom at the same time, keep notes from year to year. A camera is a good tool for keeping records of the plants in your garden, as well as recording displays in other gardens that might be adapted for yours. Then you will know for certain which bulbs can be combined.

BULBS IN LAWNS

The only bulbs that are suitable for planting in lawns are those that bloom very early, such as *Scilla*, early *Crocus* and snow drops. The foliage must have a chance to die back before the lawn is mowed. In meadow areas where the grasses can grow longer, *Camassia* and *Narcissus* work well.

FORCING BULBS

Vancouver's mild climate makes forcing bulbs an easy task. Pot up spring flowering bulbs in the fall and bury them in the garden. Under an overhang is a good spot. Dig a trench and place the pots close together. Then cover the pots with soil to a depth of four inches (10 cm). It is easier to remove the containers if perlite or peat is used rather than soil. If you do not have a garden, any cold, frost free place will work. Use the refrigerator or pack the pots in a box and insulate them with crumpled newspaper or peat moss. Place the box in a garage or in a sheltered spot on a deck. Don't forget to water them. If the forecast is for weather much below freezing, the pots will need further protection.

The bulbs will be ready to bring inside after 8 to 10 weeks of cold treatment. Place them in a dim, cool room for two weeks while the leaves develop. Once the flower stem has lengthened, the plant is given bright light to bring out the flowers.

ANNUALS - CULTIVATION

Annuals are available in the spring from garden shops to corner grocery stores. In Vancouver they seem to appear with the first whiff of spring in March, which is too early to plant out most plants. Cold hardy bedding plants such as violas, pansies, wallflowers, and primroses will be fine. Pansies and primroses are available throughout the winter and make a wonderful splash of colour. If the winter is cold, they may just sit there, waiting to bloom in February or March. A caution: they do not always survive a cold snap, particularly if in unprotected containers.

Wait before you buy other bedding plants until mid-May to June. If you can't resist a good bargain or a special cultivar, buy the plants but keep them in a cold frame until it is safe to plant them out.

When purchasing bedding plants, the cheapest is not necessarily best. Look for compact plants with foliage that looks healthy and is a good colour. Check for insects or disease. It is better to buy plants that are not in flower, because you want the plant's energy to go into getting established rather than trying to flower. If the plant has buds or flowers, nip them off. You will be rewarded with a much better display in the summer. Nurseries that grow and sell their own plants usually have top quality plants that have been fertilized and properly hardened off. Bargain plants, sold early in the season, may not have been hardened off. Plants sold in stores that are not garden-oriented may have had indifferent watering, no fertilizing and may have suffered stress.

Annuals are sold in a cell-pack, usually with four or occasionally six plants. More and more frequently, plants are sold in individual 4 inch (10 cm) pots. Plants are almost never sold in undivided flats.

GROWING FROM SEED OUTDOORS

Annuals can be seeded outdoors. It is less expensive than buying bedding plants but takes them longer to bloom. Incorporate some organic matter into the soil. Seeds must come in contact with the soil, so rake out any lumps. Sow the seeds thinly and sift a layer of soil to cover them. The soil must be kept moist until the seeds germinate. Once the seedlings have their second set of leaves, thin them out so the plants have room to grow. Some good choices for direct seeding are sweet peas, *Cosmos*, sunflowers, strawflowers, mallows and poppies.

GROWING FROM SEED INDOORS

Sowing seed indoors has the advantage of increasing your control over the growing conditions. The disadvantage is that seedlings take up a lot of space. A few seedlings can be grown on a window sill, but a home greenhouse or a room with artificial light is necessary to grow a large quantity. Home grown seedlings are certainly the answer if you are using a large number of bedding plants.

Damping-off disease (a fungus disease that attacks seedlings at soil level) is the most serious problem when growing seedlings. Use sterilized potting mixes and sow the seeds thinly to provide air circulation. Keep dead leaves picked off and always use clean tools and containers.

Use insecticidal soap if the plants get aphids or white fly. Keep a close watch on the plants. Treat an insect infestation immediately, before their numbers build up.

A week before the seedlings are to be planted out, begin to harden them off by exposing them gradually to the sun and wind. The first day, put the plants outside in the shade for an hour or two. Each day, increase the time and exposure to the sun. When planting into the garden, do it in the evening or on an overcast day. The soil in the pots should be moist so it slips easily out of the pot. If it doesn't slip out easily, turn the pot upside down and tap the rim against something hard. Disturb the roots as little as possible. Shade the plants from the sun for a few days.

Sow the seeds in sterilized seed mix. If you prefer to make your own, mix, by volume, one third peat moss, one third builder's sand or perlite and one third sterilized soil.

- Sow the seeds thinly and cover them lightly with soil.
- Water the container gently and put it into a plastic bag which will act as a mini greenhouse. Put it in a warm place until the seeds germinate. The top of the refrigerator works well.
- Once the seeds have germinated, give them light. Transplant them once they have their second set of leaves.
- To transplant or prick-out a seedling, hold it by a leaf and use a pencil to lever it out of the soil.
- Seedlings can be potted up into individual two inch (five cm) pots, flats or anything you wish as long as it has good drainage.
- Use potting soil, or mix your own. Seedlings must be kept watered and given sufficient light. Feed with half strength 20-20-20 fertilizer once a week.

> **Cold-hardy annuals can be planted out in mid-April, but wait until the last week in May to the first week in June for the tender annuals.**

Chapter 3 explains how the soil should be prepared for planting out annuals. Add compost or other organic material to improve the soil's water-holding capacity. Mulch to help conserve moisture. When preparing the soil, add a fertilizer like 6-8-6, a handful for every 10 square feet (per square metre) or 2.2 pounds (1 kg) per 12 square yards (10 square metres). Plants can be watered-in with half-strength liquid fertilizer such as 20-20-20. Fertilize at the end of June and again at the end of July.

On-going summer care includes removing dead leaves and blossoms. If annuals are allowed to set seed, they stop blooming, so plants must be dead-headed by removing spent flowers. Keep weeds pulled and water as necessary.

The pest and disease chapter (Chapter 10) deals with pests. Watch for slugs when the bedding plants are first put out. A hungry slug can eat a seedling, just as an appetizer. Controlling aphids is usually an on-going battle. Use the hose to spray them off the plants and never let the numbers build up.

In the, fall many annuals will continue to bloom until hit by a killer frost, anytime from late September until December. Once the plants have stopped blooming, remove them to the compost pile.

> **If you wish to save seeds, collect them in late August. Marigolds, impatiens and poppies are a few that set seed readily. Plants grown from saved seed will not always exactly resemble the parents. If the plant was grown from an F1 hybrid, it will not do well from seed the next year and new seed must be purchased. Seed is usually ready to harvest when the pods change colour. Store seed in a cool dry place and be sure to label the package.**

CONTAINERS

Vancouver's winters are usually mild enough that many perennials, bulbs and annuals can be grown in containers. The plants do better if the container is not too small. Small pots dry out frequently. Any container will do, from an Italian clay pot to a plastic bucket, as long as it has drain holes in the bottom. Use potting soil to plant. Drainage material in the bottom of the pot is not necessary.

Most low growing perennials grow in containers. If the container is large, some of the taller perennials will also grow successfully. Some that do well are hostas, ferns, ivies, primroses, poppies, astilbe, and many herbs.

VEGETABLE GARDENING

Vegetables are usually divided into two groups: those that do well when the weather is cool — a real boon in Vancouver since we have long, cool springs and autumns can be mild well into December — and the warm season crops.

COOL SEASON

Many vegetables do best in cooler weather, including leafy kinds such as lettuce, spinach and swiss chard; root crops like beets, carrots, radish, turnip and rutabaga; bulbous crops such as garlic, leeks and onions; legumes, including peas and broad beans; all the cole crops: broccoli, cabbage, Brussels sprouts, Chinese cabbage; asparagus, and celery.

WARM SEASON

Vancouver, with its cooler summers, is often at a disadvantage compared with the rest of the country where summer temperatures are generally hotter. Warm season vegetables originated in warm areas of the world. They are mainly grown for their fruits and seeds; examples are tomatoes, peppers, squashes, melons, cucumber, beans and corn. Many require a long growing season and are started indoors or purchased as transplants. Exceptions are bush-type beans, corn and squash, which can be sown outdoors — although squash can be started indoors to get a head start on the season. When nights become warmer, usually about June 6, it is safe to plant out most warm season plants. However, it should be safe enough to sow corn and bush-type and pole beans in mid-May.

To get a head start, these crops could go outside earlier under plastic tunnels or hot caps while the weather is cool.

LOCATION AND PLACEMENT

Please read Chapter 2 for information on the general location and placement of the vegetable garden.

Vegetables do not need to be grown in a specific area of the garden. There is nothing that says vegetables cannot be grown with annuals and perennials. Many vegetables are very attractive and are an aesthetic asset in any part of the garden. Ruby Chard, with its translucent red stems, shimmers in the sun.

Red Sails lettuce, with its attractive foliage, and eggplants with their large, attractive purple blooms can be planted among the flowers.

Vegetables can also be grown in containers if you garden in small spaces.

SHADE TOLERANT

Even if your garden has very little sun, there are vegetables that will tolerate shade: not deep shade but a semi-shaded area or one that gets sun only part of the day. Shade tolerant vegetables include lettuce, spinach, Chinese cabbage, kale and mustard greens. Radish, beet, carrots and onions are root and bulb crops that grow well, as do mint and parsley. Warm season crops need full sun for their seeds and fruit to develop.

Vegetable crops require fertile, well-drained, well-worked soil and must not be competing with tree roots and dense canopies.

PLOT SIZE

There is really no size restriction for a vegetable garden, but before you turn under the lawn, consider your needs and time. It is better to start off small and increase the size of the vegetable area as you go along. Nothing is more discouraging than to become overwhelmed, with the vegetable patch producing more weeds than food. If you have a small family, you may not need a large garden. A vegetable garden will not necessarily save you much on the grocery bill unless you process all the food not eaten fresh. Vegetables are always less expensive in the summer at the same time your garden is producing. However, nothing tastes better than fresh vegetables straight from the garden.

Although many gardeners suggest a north/south orientation for rows because each plant then gives a little shade to the next, Vancouver's cooler summers give the gardener more choice in planning. Taller plants, though, should be placed at the north end of the garden, where they will not shade other plants later in the summer.

The orientation of rows is a matter of preference. Many gardeners suggest a north/south orientation because in hot areas each plant gives a bit of shade to the next. In Vancouver, though, our summers are rarely very hot and I would plant the rows however it works best in your garden. Consider the eventual height of the plants, and place corn and the climbers like peas and beans on the north side where they will not shade other plants later in the summer.

Vegetables do not need to be placed in long single rows. Available space can be utilized to better advantage if the vegetables are planted in blocks or double and triple rows. When planted in blocks or multiple rows, less space is wasted on paths. For example, lettuce might be planted in blocks of four rows. The width of a planting is dictated by the length of your arms, since you must be able to reach to the center to weed and harvest. Corn is planted in blocks because it is pollinated by wind — a difficult process if it is planted in one long row.

Perennial vegetables such as asparagus and rhubarb are usually planted in separate beds where they will be undisturbed. Asparagus beds, once established, will last for 8 to 12 years while rhubarb will need to be divided every 5 to 7 years.

Crop rotation is an important part of vegetable gardening. There are three different groups of vegetables — the cabbage family or Brassicas, root crops, and all other vegetables — and each group has its own specific needs and pests. By not growing carrots in the same spot year after year, you help to reduce soil-borne diseases and pests. By rotating the carrots to a different spot in the vegetable garden you help to foil the insects and diseases that like carrots. When the insects or diseases that overwintered in the soil emerge, they will find a different type of vegetable growing there. Also, since different vegetables use different amounts of nutrients, by rotating the crops, annual depletion of specific plant foods is minimized.

Crop rotation is generally done on a three year cycle, but this is not a hard and fast rule. Divide the vegetable garden into three parts and add well rotted manure to one third. In this area, plant crops that produce their edible parts above the ground, such as beans, peas, celery, corn, onions and tomatoes. In the second third, add lime and plant the cole or brassica crops, including cabbage, Brussels sprouts, turnip and kale. In the last third, amend the soil with compost and plant root crops like carrots, beets, potatoes and parsnips.

Root crops tend to produce too much leaf and the roots can become multi-branched if planted after manure has been dug in. Leafy crops will benefit from the manure. Brassicas do better when the pH is higher so they are planted after the soil has been limed. Next year, treat the second third in the same manner as the first third was treated this year, and so on.

When you plan the garden, maximum use of space is a good gardening objective. To achieve this, some vegetables are planted in succession. Early lettuce and spinach might be followed by melon or squash. As lettuce is harvested, more is seeded so there will always be some ready to harvest. Crops that mature quickly, such as spring onions and radishes, are planted between slower growing vegetables where they will be harvested before the others shade them out.

Other vegetables planted in succession to extend the harvest over a longer period are bush-beans, peas, spinach and lettuce. To extend the season for cabbage and cauliflower, a selection of varieties that mature at different times is used. In Vancouver, Brussels sprouts, winter cabbage, spinach, kale and Swiss chard can be grown to harvest over the winter. These are sown in late spring or early summer and harvested in winter. The vegetables need to do their growing before the cold weather sets in. Most years, winters are mild enough that the plants are not killed but are harvestable at least until February. Some vegetables, like sprouting broccoli and winter onions, are grown for harvesting the next spring.

The amount of vegetables needed for a family is a very personal thing. Some books give lists, but generally, experience will be your best guide. Everyone has heard zucchini horror stories. It is an easy vegetable to grow, but don't despair; it will freeze if grated and it makes the best chocolate cake. Do not grow great amounts of a vegetable that the family hates but might find not so bad when eaten straight from the garden. On the other hand, it is always fun to try something new, either a new vegetable or a new variety of an old favourite.

YEAR ONE

Unit One	Unit Two	Unit Three
Well-Rotted Manure	Lime	Compost
Plants with Edible Parts	Cole or Brassica Crops	Root Crops
Above Ground	(cabbage, Brussels	(carrots, beets,
(beans, peas,celery,corn,	sprouts, turnips, kale)	potatoes,
parsnips)		

YEAR TWO

Unit One	Unit Two	Unit Three
Compost	Well-Rotted Manure	Lime
Root Crops	Plants with Edible Parts	Cole or Brassica Crops
	Above Ground	

YEAR THREE

Unit One	Unit Two	Unit Three
Lime	Compost	Well-Rotted Manure
Cole or Brassica Crops	Root Crops	Plants with Edible Parts
		Above Ground

GENERAL METHODS OF CULTIVATION

Vegetables are traditionally grown in open, flat ground. The area is dug over each spring and the vegetables are usually grown in long, straight rows. This method is still used for large scale operations that use tractors, but for the home gardener it is not always the most efficient. There is nothing wrong with open, flat gardening but over the years the soil can become compacted by walking on it.

Consider making permanent narrow beds so the same paths are used year after year. The top soil from the path area is piled on top of the growing area leaving the path slightly lower than the garden.

> **Beds should be no wider than can comfortably be reached at the middle for weeding. Use any convenient length. Only the beds are dug and they should not be walked on. If it is necessary to walk on a bed, stand on a board to distribute your weight.**

Raised beds are a variation on the narrow beds. Wood or bricks are used to make permanent beds which can vary in height from eight inches (20 cm) to waist height. Raised beds are a boon when bending is difficult. They are attractive, and weeding never seems to be as great a problem —all in the mind, I'm sure! Slugs are not as prevalent in raised beds, which is a real plus on the coast. Depending on the height of the bed, you could sit on the edge to work. We can have rain until late June or early July, and raised beds drain well and warm up fast in the spring. This is also an advantage in areas where the water table is high.

The disadvantages of raised beds are the cost of building them and the extra soil needed to fill them. However, only the top 11 inches (27.5 cm) need to be really good soil.

SOIL

For general information, please see Chapter 3 — Soil Improvement.

Vegetables grow in many types of soil, even poor soil, after a fashion. But to produce tasty vegetables, the soil should be as good as you can make it. Each year, dig in a four inch (10 cm) layer of compost and sow a green manure crop in late summer to early fall (see Chapter 3 for recommended green manure crops). With care, the soil will improve gradually each year, and if you are lucky and already have good soil, amending it each year will keep it good.

Soil can also be amended with other organic materials such as mushroom manure or seaweed, which are readily available in Vancouver.

If you are buying top soil, buy it from a reputable dealer to be sure it is of good quality.

Animal manure may be available. It should be put on the garden in the fall or composted for a season if not well aged. Fresh manure will burn plant roots.

The amount of nutrients that are added with manure and compost will vary and most gardens will require additional fertilizer. A good all purpose fertilizer to use in Vancouver is 6-8-6. Add it to the soil at planting, a handful to the square metre, and again at intervals for vegetables that have a long growing season. Celery, for example, could be watered with a solution of liquid fertilizer (diluted according to the instructions on the package) every two weeks during the growing season. Vegetables can be side-dressed with a granular fertilizer when they are growing. The fertilizer is scattered in a narrow band alongside the row, a handful to every ten sqare feet (one square metre). Do not let the fertilizer touch the stem or leaves, because it will burn them.

SEED BED PREPARATION

Once the soil is dug and weed free, rake the bed to break up and crumble the lumps of soil. Then smooth the bed with the back of the rake. A fine textured, level seed bed is important, since seeds must be in contact with the soil to germinate. If great lumps are left, germination will be spotty as some of the seeds fall into deep cracks and others hang in air pockets.

The soil must be weed and debris free. Weeds rob the vegetables of nutrients, water and light. If you try to grow onions for instance, and do not weed, your yield will be reduced by 80 per cent, and that's a lot of onions.

SEED SOWING METHODS

Drill Sowing   If the garden is flat and the seeds are planted in long rows, drill sowing is used. After preparing the seed bed, place a stake with a long string attached to it in the ground at one end of the proposed row. Place another stake at the other end, attaching the string to it. The string needs to be taut since it is used as a guide in keeping the seed drill straight. Using the corner of a hoe or a blunt stick, draw a shallow trench in the soil surface following the length of the string. After sowing, be sure to permanently mark the ends of each row. It's easy to forget what and where you have sown when sowing over several days and weeks.

Water the seed drill before the seed is sown to ensure the seed is in contact with damp soil. This is essential for germination.

Seeds must be sown thinly. Most seed packages give a guideline of the number of seeds to sow. If seeds are small they can be mixed with sand, making it easier to sow thinly. Once germinated, if they are not crowded, it will be easier to thin them to the correct spacing.

Seeds must be sown at the correct depth, usually shown on the seed package. If seeds are sown too deeply they may not germinate. Some seeds, like lettuce and celery, need some light to germinate and if they are covered with soil too deeply, germinate poorly. Covering the seeds with fine soil, sand or vermiculite will ensure good contact with the seed.

Station Sowing   Larger seeds may be sown initially at the correct final spacing. To avoid gaps in the row, three or four seeds are placed together at the required intervals. Once the seeds have germinated, all but the strongest seedling are nipped out. Excess seedlings are usually removed by pinching or cutting the stem rather than pulling. This prevents disturbing the roots of the seedling that is left to grow on.

A variation on this method works particularly well with vegetables like beets and onions that will sprawl sideways as they grow. If the final spacing is six inches (15 cm), plant three or four seeds every 12 inches (30 cm). The seedlings are not thinned, and they will push out sideways and grow well, even if they are crowded, because of the greater space between each group of plants.

Dibble Sowing   A dibble is a nice English tool. It is a smooth piece of polished wood like a thick pencil, which is used to make holes in the soil for individual large seeds like squash or melons. Personally, I find my index finger works just as well and I never lose it. Up to the first knuckle is about one inch (2.5 cm).

After the hole is made, set the seed in the bottom and cover it with soil. A few extra seeds can be sown at the end of the row to transplant into any gaps.

COVERING SEEDS TO SPEED UP GERMINATION

There are several ways to help speed up germination in the spring when the weather and soil are cool. Traditionally in France, large glass jars that looked like bells were placed over individual plants to act as miniature greenhouses. Today we can recycle plastic milk jugs. Cut off the bottoms and place them over planted seeds that are well spaced. Plastic hot caps can be purchased to do the same thing. When seed rows are sown closer together, plastic tunnels can be purchased or made by covering hoops of wire shoved into the soil with clear plastic or slit plastic mesh. The plastic is left on until the weather warms but beware; if the sun is hot, the sides of clear plastic tunnels will need to be rolled up during the day once the seeds have germinated.

> **Plastic coverings warm up the soil and effectively extend the season, allowing you to plant earlier.**

Clear plastic, placed directly on the soil a week before seeds are planted, will warm it. Plant the seeds through slits. A disadvantage with this method is that the weeds germinate, too. To reduce problems, lift the plastic after the weeds have sprouted and remove them before you sow your seeds. In theory the hot sun should kill the tiny weed seedlings as they germinate. I suspect the reason this doesn't work in Vancouver is because we often have cloudy days and there is not enough sun to kill the weeds. The research station at Cloverdale found that black plastic did not work well to warm the soil.

Since it holds a lot of moisture, soil that contains a lot of organic material will be slower to warm in the spring. If you have topped the soil with mulch, pull it back a few inches from where the seed is to be planted.

In the heat of summer if seeds are slow to germinate, cover the row with a board to keep the soil cooler and prevent it from drying out. Check each day. Remove the boards as soon as the seeds have germinated.

WET OR COLD SOILS

It is really important not to walk on wet soil because this causes the soil to compact, making it difficult for roots to grow, thereby reducing yields. Place a board where you must walk to plant the seeds. This will distribute your weight and result in less damage to the soil structure. Make a long narrow v-shaped drill to the correct depth for the seeds being sown. Cover the drill with a cloche or clear plastic for a few days prior to sowing to warm and dry out the seed drill.

Dry peat moss could be placed in the bottom of the drill to help soak up the extra moisture. If you have a high water table in your area, consider raised beds, which will warm up and dry out faster in the spring.

DRY SOIL AND WEATHER

Dry soil and weather are not a spring problem on the coast, but summers are predictably dry. To help your seeds germinate during the warmer weather, make a seed drill as above and water it well with a watering can with a narrow spout. Sow the seeds and cover them with dry soil and a board to slow down the evaporation. Remember to check under the board frequently and remove it when the seeds germinate.

FLUID SOWING

This is a sowing method used frequently in the United Kingdom. It is fun to try at home, but it is usually used for large scale commercial planting. It speeds up growth and ensures evenly spaced plants without misses in the row because only seeds that have already germinated are planted. It promotes earlier growth, development and harvesting than if the seeds are sown in the traditional manner.

Step one is to pre-germinate the seeds. Sprinkle them on moist blotting or other absorbent paper and place them in a warm spot at a temperature of about 70°F (21°C). As soon as the roots begin to emerge from the seed, mix them with a thick gel of dilute, non-fungicidal wallpaper paste. A warning — the root must be no more than barely showing or it can break off during sowing. If you are unable to sow the seeds immediately, put them in the refrigerator until you can sow them. This should be for no more than a day or two.

Put the mixture in a plastic bag and cut one corner. Make the initial cut small and enlarge it if the gel does not squeeze out evenly. Slowly squeeze a stream out of the bag along the bottom of the seed drill and cover with soil.

BROADCAST SOWING

When seeds are broadcast sown, they are scattered over the soil rather than individually planted. Lawn seed and green manure crops are broadcast. This is not usually a very efficient way to sow vegetables, although it will work in small areas. The secret is to sow the seeds thinly and distribute them evenly over the area. Rake the soil lightly to cover the seeds and water them in with a gentle spray. Once the seeds have germinated, thin them to the correct distance. The area sown must be small or narrow enough so that weeding and thinning can be done without walking in the bed.

Fluid sowing (usually used for large scale commercial planting, rather than home gardening) speeds up growth and ensures evenly spaced plants.

THINNING OUT SEEDLINGS

One of the major reasons vegetables, or for that matter any plants sown from seed, fail is because they were not thinned or not thinned soon enough. Some vegetables such as bunching onions, scallions, radishes and bunching carrots are not thinned out but thinly sown and harvested when immature. Other vegetables are grown and allowed to mature where they are sown but need to be thinned to the correct distance to produce full sized crops.

As soon as the seedlings are large enough to handle, the surplus is removed, leaving the remaining seedlings far enough apart to develop fully and mature. For some crops, optimum production is achieved by thinning out in stages. For example, if mature lettuce are spaced 12 inches (30 cm) apart, first thin them to stand three inches (7.5 cm) apart. When the young plants touch, remove and use alternate plants, leaving the remainder six inches (15 cm) apart. Finally, again remove and use alternate plants, leaving those remaining to fully mature.

When thinning rows, the soil should be damp to minimize the shock to the remaining plants. If the plants are watered the day before, the soil should be just right. Be sure to firm up the soil around the remaining seedlings and give them a good watering after you have thinned. When the seedlings are small, they can be nipped out with your fingernails rather than being pulled so the roots of the adjoining plants are not disturbed.

If mature enough when you thin them, the plants could be eaten in a salad or transplanted to fill gaps in the row. Generally, root crops do not transplant well because once the tip of a tap root is broken the root will split.

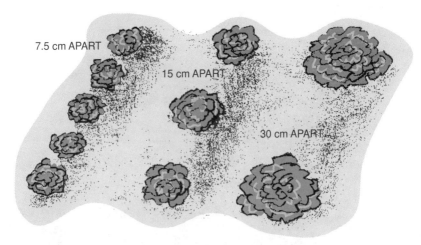

7.5 cm APART

15 cm APART

30 cm APART

Lettuce is thinned when the plants are immature. The soil should be damp when you are thinning, to minimize the shock to the remaining plants. Firm up the soil around remaining seedlings, and use the thinned plants in a salad.

Many warm season vegetables, such as tomatoes, peppers and eggplants, require a longer growing season than our weather permits. To get around this we use transplants. These are small plants raised from seed that have been grown inside a sunny window or greenhouse. Transplants are already growing well when they are put into the garden in June. Cool weather vegetables can also be started inside to get a jump on the season.

You can start seeds inside or purchase transplants from garden centres or even the local grocery store. If you are raising many plants and have the space, it is more economical to grow them yourself. If you need only a few plants it may be more convenient to purchase them. One problem with buying warm season plants in Vancouver is they are often available far too early, up to two months before it is safe for them to be planted out. If it is a variety you particularly want you should buy the plant when you see it, but it must be kept inside during cool weather until the nights are warm. When seedlings have to be held in the house until it is safe to plant them out, it is difficult to give them the best growing conditions. The plants may get leggy due to insufficient light and may need to be potted on into larger containers several times. If the roots are restricted in too small a pot, the plants will be set back and not do as well.

Be wary of transplants of cole crops, such as cabbage, cauliflower and Brussels sprouts, unless they were grown in artificial media. There is a chance of introducing the disease club root into your garden, and it remains in soil for many years.

Because of Vancouver's relatively short growing season, transplants are used when growing warm season vegetables like tomatoes and peppers.

RAISING FROM SEED OUTDOORS

In most cases, seed that is sown outdoors is sown in a permanent row; however, a nursery bed could be used to raise seedlings like salad and cole crops for transplanting into the main garden later. This method might be used to have plants ready to succeed other vegetables as harvested. This will insure faster maturity of later crops.

Managing a seed bed is the same as planting directly. The soil should be finely raked. Since the plants will be removed as seedlings, the rows may be closer together. The seedlings will still need to be thinned to give the young plants growing room and not stunt their development.

RAISING FROM SEED INDOORS

Generally, the warm season crops are the ones raised indoors but cole and salad vegetables can also be started indoors. The limitations to raising seeds indoors are on light, temperature, space and time. Generally root crops, peas, beans and corn are not started as transplants. Chapter 5 deals with raising annuals from seed. Vegetables require similar care.

PURCHASING SEEDLINGS FROM A NURSERY

Most vegetables that nurseries sell are sold as seedlings. An exception is asparagus, which is sold as two year old, bare root plants. Also, rhubarb crowns and potato and Jerusalem artichoke tubers are sold. The plants should look fresh and not have broken roots. They should be planted out as soon as purchased. If this is not possible, do not let the roots dry out. In the case of tubers, store them in a cool, dark place until planted.

Sometimes vegetables are sold as individual plants in containers. If the container is large they may be left in it and grown on a patio. Plants in smaller containers need to be planted into the garden at the appropriate time. A warm weather vegetable would not go outside until June, but a hardy plant like cabbage could go out in April.

Container grown vegetables should be compact and have fresh green leaves.

Roots should not be circling the bottom of the container.

Never buy plants that have yellowed leaves or any sign of pests or disease.

Vegetables that have been kept in the same container for too long may never recover satisfactorily.

TRANSPLANTING TECHNIQUE

Asparagus and rhubarb are the only bare rooted vegetables sold here. They should be placed in prepared beds. Since they are perennial, and the plants — as in the case of asparagus — may be there many years, the bed must have organic matter dug in.

Container grown vegetables should be hardened off before, and protected from the sun for several days after, planting out. Overcast days are great for putting out transplants. Usually if you wait a day or so the weather will cooperate.

If the container is made of peat it can be planted without removing the plant, but be sure it is covered with soil. If the top of the container sticks up above soil level, it will act as a wick and draw moisture away from the roots. If the transplants are small use a dibble to make the hole, but a trowel is handy for larger plants. Firm the soil and water in the plants immediately after planting.

TYPES OF CROPS

POTATOES

Early potatoes are planted from mid-March through April. Later varieties can be planted up to mid-June. Plant them in a trench six inches (15 cm) deep and space the plants 12 inches (30 cm) apart with 15 inches (37.5 cm) between the rows. Use small whole seed potatoes if they are available. They do not need to be cut, which will mean there is less chance of disease. If larger tubers are used, cut them so that each piece has an eye. Allow the cut surfaces to dry and harden. Plant the eye upper-most. Potato plants are not thinned or started as transplants.

If the soil is well enriched no further fertilizer will be needed. Do not add too much fertilizer because you will get more leaves than potatoes. As the plants grow, mound soil or straw up around them. The tubers form along underground stems. They must not be exposed to the sun. Keep the plants well watered.

Early potatoes can be harvested once the plant flowers. Try removing the tiny potatoes without disturbing the whole plant. Remove enough for dinner. New potatoes do not keep well and are best eaten within a few days of harvesting. Potatoes are harvested in the late summer through fall.

Store potatoes in a dark, frost free place.

A common potato problem is soil borne scab disease. The name is very descriptive of the symptoms, as the skin develops corky, wart-like growths. The potatoes are still edible, just peel the skin off. Avoid using lime where potatoes are to be grown.

ARTICHOKES

Globe artichokes are large, perennial plants that do not always survive our winters, but there are varieties that can be grown from seed. Start the plants indoors from February to mid-March and plant them out at the beginning of May. The plants need a fair amount of room so leave two feet between plants and three feet between rows. They are heavy feeders so dig well rotted manure into the soil. Artichokes are sturdy plants and will not need staking. They are ready to harvest in late August. In the late fall, cut back the plant and mulch it heavily. If the winter is mild it might survive. Nurseries carry plants in the spring for transplanting into the garden. Black aphids are a real pest and they will need to be controlled quickly.

JERUSELEM ARTICHOKES

These are a North American native only distantly related to the globe artichoke. The tubers are harvested rather than the flower. These plants are tall and could become weedy if the tubers are not harvested each year. Plant the tubers in the early spring six inches (15 cm) deep and 18 inches (45 cm) apart. Rake in some 6-8-6 before they are planted. The soil should be well drained. They will need to be watered in the summer when it is dry.

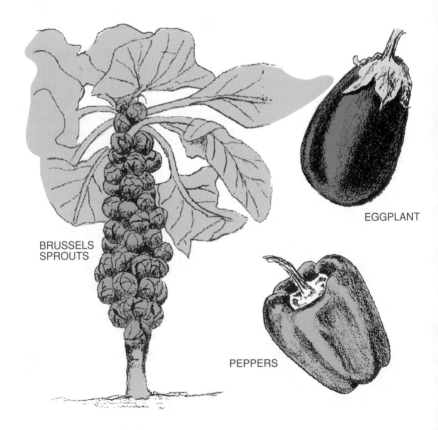

EGGPLANT

BRUSSELS
SPROUTS

PEPPERS

They can be harvested throughout the winter as long as the soil is not frozen. The ground is a perfect storage site.

COLE OR BRASSICA CROPS

These are cold weather vegetables. There are many varieties, including winter cabbage, Brussels sprouts, sprouting broccoli and kale, that will withstand most of our winters. Others are grown and harvested over the spring and summer. The coles can be grown as transplants or sown directly. Either method works well and should be dictated by your indoor growing space. If you plan your garden, you can have some type of cole crop to eat almost twelve months of the year. Most of the brassicas can be sown in succession to extend the season. One exception is Brussels sprouts, which need to be sown in early summer to be ready for harvesting next winter.

There is such a large variety of coles that each one will have different spacing in the garden. Check the seed package for individual crops, but generally the seeds are planted 1/2 inch (1.25 cm) deep and the plants are thinned to 12 to 18 inches (30 to 45 cm) apart with two to three feet (60 to 90 cm) between the rows.

The Imported cabbage butterfly is the biggest pest on these crops. Try covering the rows with Reemay, a reusable white material which allows water and air through but keeps out the insects and prevents eggs from being laid on the leaves.

ROOT CROPS

Root crops grow best in good, well drained garden soil that has been enriched with compost and is free of stones. Avoid fresh manure as it has a tendency to cause forked and hairy roots. Use 6-8-6 or another balanced fertilizer when the seeds are sown. Dig the soil deeply, especially for parsnips and carrots because the roots have a tendency to split in compacted soil that is difficult to push through.

Turnips and beets will grow easily. Both the root and young leaves are edible. Rutabagas take a month longer to grow than the smaller turnip. They are rougher looking and stronger flavoured. Carrots and parsnips are also root crops. Parsnips and late carrots are left in the ground for winter harvest since their flavour will improve after a frost.

Root crops are all cool weather crops. They can be sown in succession from April through mid-July. Sow the seeds 1/2 to 3/4 inch (1 to 2 cm) deep and sift some fine soil over the seeds to help the seedlings emerge as they germinate. Gradually thin carrots, turnips and beets, pulling every second one. The small thinnings can be eaten in salads. Generally root crops are not transplanted but sown directly.

If you have a problem with the soil borne disease scab, avoid using lime on these crops and do not plant them immediately after growing a potato crop, which is also susceptible to the organism which causes this disease.

Carrots, and occasionally parsnips, can have a problem with carrot rust fly which makes rusty red channels in the root. Cover the carrots with Reemay to stop the fly from laying its eggs, and rotate all crops each year.

LEAFY SALAD CROPS

Leafy vegetables like lettuce, spinach, arugula and endive do well on the coast with our cool, damp springs. If you have a cold frame, you can start lettuce as early as February or March and can continue to have fresh greens through to October or later depending on the weather. Leafy vegetables are easy to grow and adapt well to containers if you do not have a garden.

Grow them in good garden soil with a balanced fertilizer. Sow the seeds 1/2 inch (1.25 cm) deep and gradually thin the plants to 12 inches (30 cm) or so apart depending on the vegetable. Crowded plants will be poor in quality and are prone to rotting. Adequate water is a must because the growth needs to be continuous or the plants become bitter.

There are many interesting greens to be grown and some are very cold hardy, such as spinach, corn salad and arugula. Some of the greens have a pungent flavour and are tasty when mixed with other greens. For the most delicate flavour, pick the leaves when they are small. Sow these greens in the late summer as they will bolt -- elongate, flower and set seed --when the weather is too hot.

CUCURBITS

This is a warm weather family of vegetables which originated in countries like South America and India. They will languish or die if put out in the garden too soon. Sow the seeds or set out transplants in early June. Raised beds and soil that has been covered with plastic will warm up more quickly. Spacing is important as many of the plants require a fair amount of room. The smaller cucumbers and squash that do not scramble, or crawl across the ground or up a trellis, will take up less space, needing only three feet (90 cm) between plants, while the large pumpkins or winter squash need 10 feet (3 metres). Cucumbers will scramble up a trellis as well as sprawl. This family does well in rich soil and will happily grow on top of a compost pile.

The slower maturing winter squash and pumpkins need to be fertilized several times over the growing season. All varieties need a basic fertilizer at planting time.

Cucumbers and summer squash should be picked often as the fruit can quickly become too large and less tasty. These plants are prolific and a few plants will provide enough for a family.

Generally these plants are not pruned, but once pumpkins have set their fruit some gardeners prefer to remove the ends of the vines. I do not prune them because the cut is an entry way for disease and the leaves are needed to manufacture food for the plant. However, if you are growing a giant pumpkin allow only one well established fruit on each plant.

Summer squash and cucumbers are eaten fresh, pickled or used in baking. Winter squash are harvested before a heavy frost and stored at 50°- 60° F (10°-15° C), unlike most vegetables, which are stored at near-freezing temperatures.

TOMATOES, PEPPERS AND EGGPLANTS

The tomato is grown by most gardeners. Like peppers and eggplants, it is a warm weather vegetable. All are suitable for containers and are ornamental looking, particularly eggplants and peppers. If the vegetable garden is small, put them in the flower garden among the annuals and perennials.

They should not be planted outside until the end of the first week in June, although they can go out earlier in a cold frame or under plastic. They require a long growing season and plants need to be started indoors. Most years, tomatoes do well, but large beef steak tomatoes are usually disappointing in our cool summers.

Tomatoes are started six to eight weeks before they are planted out, peppers twelve to fourteen weeks and eggplants eight weeks. Start the seeds on top of the refrigerator or another warm spot and do not let the young seedlings get chilled, which will set them back. As the plants grow they will need to be potted up into larger pots so their growth isn't interrupted.

Heat loving vegetables must be planted in full sun in well-drained, loamy soil. Mulching the plants will help to conserve moisture and prevent blossom end rot which is prevalent on tomatoes. It is a deficiency caused by the unavailability of calcium when moisture in the soil fluctuates greatly.

The ultimate spacing in the garden will vary depending on the variety of plant.

Peppers and eggplants will not need to be staked. Tomatoes are usually staked or grown in cages unless they are small varieties which might be allowed to tumble over the edge of a tub or basket.

Tomatoes are one of the few vegetables that are pruned. This involves removing the side shoots or suckers that form in the junction of the stem and leaf stalk. They are rubbed off as they form. One or two near the bottom of the plant can be allowed to grow, giving the plant two or three main stems, or all can be removed leaving a single main stem. Pick the fruits as they mature.

Do not let the eggplants get too large as they are very tasty when four or five inches (10 or 12 cm) long and not too fat.

Tomatoes, peppers and eggplants can be stored for a few days in the refrigerator. Both tomatoes and peppers can be frozen or used in pickles. At the end of the growing season, tomato plants can be pulled up and hung in a cool basement. The tomatoes on the plant will continue to ripen.

ONIONS AND LEEKS

Onions and leeks do well in our climate. Although they grow best in the sun, they will tolerate light shade. Onion sets are readily available in the stores in the spring.

They will give you almost instant onions and are easy to plant. If you grow shallots, save some small bulbs to use as sets for next year. Onions are also easy to grow from seed. The larger sweet onions are started indoors in February while other varieties are sown directly in the ground from April through May. Onions can be sown in single rows, but to maximize space sow them in bands of four rows. Gradually thin the seedlings, pulling every second onion until they are spaced about three inches (7.5 cm) apart in all directions. Use the thinnings for salads. Do not leave them lying between the rows because the onion scent will attract the onion fly. Its larvae damage onion bulbs.

Take advantage of our mild winters and sow onions like Sweet Winter in late August for an early spring harvest.

Leeks are sown indoors in March for the earlier maturing varieties or directly sown in the ground in May. The later sown leeks are harvested after the frost and will keep well in the ground during the early part of the winter. Most leeks will not survive a severe frost.

Transplants are set in an eight inch (20 cm) wide trough. The soil is back-filled in as the plants grow. They can also be set at ground level and the soil mounded around them as they grow. Seeds are sown 1/2 inch (1.25 cm) deep and thinned to four inches (10 cm) apart.

Onions and leeks should be hand weeded because the roots are shallow and could be damaged with a hoe.

Onions are harvested when the tips of the leaves turn brown. The leaves usually fall over, which helps the plants to harden off and improves their keeping quality. Sweet onions and pickling onions should be used immediately. Cooking onions and shallots, after they have been pulled and allowed to dry for a few days, will keep most of the winter.

CORN

Corn is a warm season crop that is not planted until the soil warms up from mid-May through June. Corn needs full sun and should be fertilized at sowing time and then side dressed in a month by sprinkling fertilizer beside the plants along the row, and again when the ears are forming. Plant corn in blocks because it is wind pollinated. Long single rows will not be pollinated efficiently.

Corn is sown directly outdoors, one inch (2.5 cm) deep and thinned to 10 inches (25 cm). Corn is another shallow rooted crop and care is needed when weeding. To get a jump on the season, it may be sown three weeks early and covered with clear plastic until the plants are ready to thin.

Corn is ready to harvest when the husks have darkened and the ears have filled out. Newer varieties of corn are sweeter and will keep longer in storage than the older varieties but are still best eaten as soon as possible after harvest.

HERBS

Herbs do well in Vancouver, and most winters are mild enough that you can pop outside for a bit of parsley. Annual herbs such as borage, dill and basil are sown each year. Many herbs are perennial and several, including bee balm, chives, mint, fennel and thyme, are attractive enough to go in the flower garden. Many herbs do well in containers. Some, like the ground hugging thymes, make good ground covers, and others, like the tall feather bronze fennel, make dramatic backdrop foils for other plants in the perennial bed. Try a hanging basket or tub of herbs near the kitchen door for easy pickings.

Most herbs are easily grown from seed. Alternatively, buy plants in the spring from the nurseries or the herb stands at Granville Island. A word of warning about mints: they spread, so sink a bottomless bucket into the ground and plant the mint in the bucket. They could also be planted in containers.

Herbs do best in full sun and fertile soil, although some, like borage, will tolerate poorer soils.

Harvesting of fresh young leaves, seeds and stems depends on the herb. The plants are used fresh, frozen or dried and stored in air tight bottles or plastic bags.

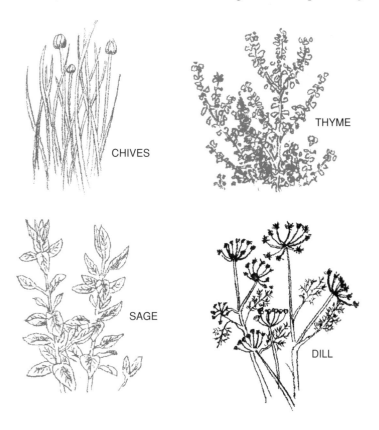

CHIVES

THYME

SAGE

DILL

CHAPTER 7
FRUIT GROWING

Plants that produce fruit fall into several categories. Stone fruits are those that have a pit or stone surrounded by edible flesh, like plums and cherries. Pome fruits are apples, pears and quince. Blueberries, currants and gooseberries are bush fruits. Brambles are shrubs that produce long canes that scramble along the ground and over bushes, such as blackberry, tayberry and raspberry — all of which are members of the *Rubus* family, like our native June berries. Brambles, bushfruit, kiwi, grapes and strawberries are often called soft fruits. Vines include grapes and kiwi.

LOCATION AND PLACEMENT

PLOT SIZE AND VOLUME

Most city gardeners do not have space for an orchard, so generally the fruit trees we choose must be placed about the garden. Bush fruits, particularly blueberries, are very attractive shrubs and an asset in the landscape.

Apple trees on dwarfing rootstocks should be used since they take up less space, fruiting when young. Apple trees are the main variety grafted on to dwarfing rootstocks, but there are also some naturally dwarf fruit trees that do not need a dwarfing rootstock to keep them small. Dwarf fruit trees need eight to ten feet (2.5 to 3 m) of space between trees while cherry trees need 20 feet (six m) and pears, plums and peaches 15 feet (4.5 m).

Most gardens will only have room for a few trees and each family's choice of fruit trees and shrubs will differ according to their tastes. The number of trees grown could be increased if you espalier them. Espalier trees are trained to grow two dimensionally along wires or a wall. They can also be trained to grow along a walk-way or at knee height in front of a bed.

LAYOUT AND SPACING

Chapter 2 discusses garden planning, which will help you decide how to place fruit trees in your garden. All fruit trees and shrubs will need full sun, a minimum of six hours per day at mid-summer, and space to grow well. If plants are too crowded they will be competing with others for nutrients, water and light. Brambles take too much space if allowed to sprawl, so they must have a post, trellis or fence to be trained against.

Raspberries are grown commercially in and around Vancouver. Growers use a "T"-shaped support at each end of the row. Several wires are stretched from the top of one "T" to the other, supporting the canes as they grow. Space raspberries 15 inches (30 cm) apart in the row.

Blackberries and other brambles can be tied along a fence. The new growth is left on the ground during the summer, then lifted and tied to the fence after harvesting when the old fruited canes have been removed.

Kiwi vines require a sturdy trellis because they are very heavy. Both a male and a female plant are needed. Grapes are trained over an arbour or on wires stretched between six foot (1.8 m) fence posts. Usually two wires are used, the first wire half way up the post and the other wire at the top. Two canes are trained along the top and two along the lower wire.

Strawberries are usually planted in a bed on their own and will need to be replanted every three or four years, preferably in a different site to reduce disease problems.

Raspberries will take too much space if allowed to sprawl, so they are grown on 'T'-shaped supports. Grape vines are trained on wires stretched between six foot fence posts.

PROTECTION

Vancouver is blessed with mild winters and cool summers, which are great for growing fruit. Some winters are harder than others on the plants. Kiwis can be damaged by wind and cold and will grow better if they are sheltered. Most of the fruit trees are fine during the cold but the early flowering cherry crop is sometimes affected if there is a cold spell when they are in bloom. When Vancouver has snow it can be very wet and heavy. Gently brush it off branches to prevent them from breaking. In cold winters, strawberries will benefit from mulching, but generally it is not done. If you live on a windy, exposed site, a shelter belt of trees would be an advantage, or take advantage of the shelter from buildings and fences. Avoid planting fruit trees in frost pockets (low areas in the garden where heavier cold air drains) as a late frost could affect the buds.

POLLINATION — CULTIVARS

Many fruit trees must be cross-pollinated for mature fruit to set. Cross-pollination occurs when the eggs or ova in the female reproductive organs of the flowers are fertilized by pollen from the male reproductive organs or anthers from a different variety (cultivar) of the same or similar type of fruit.

Most apple and pear trees need a cross-pollinator, which means at least two different varieties of each must be grown, and in the case of some apple varieties that have poor pollen set, three different cultivars are needed. If a neighbour has a suitable tree it could act as the pollinator, but if possible it is better not to rely on a tree that could be removed.

Some apples to consider are Transparent, an early summer apple, and Tydeman's Red, which is partially self-fertile but will produce a better crop if cross-pollinated. Some other good choices are Gravenstein, Spartan, and Jonagold but they all need a cross-pollinator.

Some pears to grow on the coast are Bartlett, D'Anjou, Clapp Favourite and 20th Century Pear, which is often called an apple-pear. All need a cross-pollinator. Bartlett is a good choice because it will act as a pollinator for most other pears.

Cherries have complicated requirements, and not only do you need two different varieties but they must be compatible. Choose a self-fertile tree such as the compact Stella. It is a universal pollen donor for other cherry trees, fruiting without the aid of another variety. Sweet cherry trees are big but if you have room, try growing a Bing with a Van or a Sam. Sour cherries do not need a cross-pollinator and two varieties are Montmorency and North Star, which is naturally a semi-dwarf.

Prune plums do well in Vancouver and will set a better crop if cross-pollinated with another plum like Bradshaw, Greengage or Damson

Peaches and nectarines (genetically, peaches without fuzz) are self-pollinating. Try growing Redhaven, Canadian Wonder, a genetic dwarf, or Fairhaven. Redgold is a good nectarine.

Apricots do not do well in Vancouver.

Blueberries are self-pollinating but produce better if several different varieties are grown, which can also yield over a longer period of time. Some varieties that do well in Vancouver are Early Blue, Blueray and Bluecrop.

Other small fruits are self-pollinating so you will only need one variety of each.

Gooseberries and currants produce well here, as do figs — in a sheltered spot — and medlars and quince. They do not need to be cross-pollinated.

SOIL

Strawberries, raspberries, blueberries and cranberries, as well as some of the less common fruits like currants and gooseberries, are grown commercially in and near Vancouver. Grapes and kiwi are grown on a small scale. Fruit trees are often grown commercially, although in the Vancouver area they are generally grown only in home gardens. The above fruits grow best in Vancouver. Our acidic soil is especially suited to cranberry and blueberry production.

Fruit trees grow best in deep, well-drained loam, ideally about seven feet (two metres) deep with a well-draining subsoil below. The water table should be at least three feet (one metre) below the soil surface. If the water table is higher, the soil could be mounded into raised beds. Fruit trees can be grown in half barrels. The pH should not be extreme in either direction, but preferably slightly acidic. Fruit trees will grow with a pH range of 5-8. (See Chapter 3 for pH information.)

SOIL PREPARATION

Chapter 3 deals with general soil preparation. The soil should be free of weeds that compete with the young trees for nutrients and water and harbour disease and insect pests. Weeds can also provide a hiding place for rodents that dine on the bark. Amend the soil with compost to improve the soil structure. Fresh manure should not be added because it can burn tender roots. Do not add fertilizer at planting or in the first growing year. It is a good idea to have the soil tested. In subsequent years, fruit trees and bushes are fertilized in the spring.

If all the fruit trees and shrubs are planted in one area, the soil could be amended over the whole area, but for most people, the plants will be going into either an existing landscape or will be used as ornamentals as well as for their fruit. If a tree is placed in a lawn, remove the grass in a three foot (one metre) diameter circle around the trunk to reduce competition. Be careful not to over fertilize the lawn as it will also affect the tree.

When the hole is dug and the soil amended, do not leave the sides of the hole with starkly different types of soil. Slightly enlarge the hole, mixing some of the amended soil into its sides, making a transition area so that roots will be able to move easily from one soil texture to another.

PURCHASING PLANTS

The best selection of fruit plants is available in the spring when all bare rooted plants are on the market. Bare rooted trees should be dormant, without any leaves. Strawberries are usually sold in bundles of ten or so. They are bare rooted, but unlike trees they have a few small leaves.

> **Bare rooted stock should be planted immediately. If this is not possible, heel the plants in by placing them in a shallow trench and covering the roots with soil. Do not let the roots dry out. Keep the soil moist.**

Balled and burlap trees are available mainly in the spring. They should be treated like bare rooted plants. The burlap will eventually break down, although very slowly. If the root ball is solid, carefully remove the burlap, as much as possible, before the soil is back-filled in.

When purchasing plants, buy from reputable dealers. Check the plants to be sure they look healthy. They should not have broken branches and the graft union (where appropriate) should look healthy and secure. The graft union is where the tree cultivar or scion is joined to the rootstock. If plants are in leaf, leaves must be free from pests and disease and be a good colour. Roots should not be circling the bottom but should fill the container. Plants that have just been potted up will not have a well developed root system and will have a harder time when planted out. Plants should be clearly labeled.

PLANTING

There are two kinds of container grown plants: true container grown and containerized.

Container Grown   This is a plant grown in a container for one or more growing seasons. Its root-soil ball has absolute integrity and may be removed from the container without breaking up or any soil dropping off.

Container grown plants can be safely planted any time the soil is not frozen. The summer is the least favourable season because the heat is hard on newly planted plants.

Containerized   This is a plant potted in a container in late fall or early spring which has grown in it for less than one complete growing season. Depending on how long a plant has been in a container, the integrity of its root-soil ball may range from good to nil. If there is little integrity, the root-soil ball may totally or partially break apart when the plant is removed from the container. The plant may subsequently die or be seriously set back.

If the container is plastic or metal, it may be wise to leave the plant in it for several months before planting to allow time for the root-soil ball to develop sufficient integrity to permit planting.

Remove the container before planting, even if it is a biodegradable fibre pot. They often take a long time to degrade and will restrict new root growth. The sides of the container can be slit in at least four places to make it easier to remove. Maintain the soil in a moist but not soggy condition throughout the growing season.

If you plan on training an espalier tree, buy a one year old whip (a grafted fruit tree that has not leafed out) or a two year old plant. These are not easy to find, but nurseries should be able to order them. There is a nursery on Westham Island that specializes in espaliers.

CULTURAL PRACTICES

ROOTSTOCKS

Rootstocks are used to graft the desirable cultivar onto. Grafting is the joining of a cultivar (a named horticultural variety) to a rootstock that adds its desirable characteristics (such as earlier fruiting, hardiness, disease resistance or smaller size) to the cultivar that is grafted onto it. The tree is cut six inches (15 cm) to one foot (30 cm) from the roots and the desired cultivar is cut on the same angle and tied into place. Once the two pieces are joined, if the graft takes, the desired cultivar will grow in the intended way. Each rootstock has advantages and disadvantages.

A full sized tree is called a standard; a semi-standard is 70 per cent of a full sized tree; semi-dwarf is 50 per cent the size of a standard and a dwarf is 30 per cent.

POME FRUIT

Apples are rarely grown on their own roots. The cultivar or variety is grafted onto a rootstock. The main apple rootstocks used are numbered. The most frequent ones used in Vancouver are, in order of their dwarfing qualities, M27 which grows to about six feet (1.8 m), M9 to 9 feet (2.7 m) and M26 to 12 feet (3.6 m). Trees on M27, M9 and M26 rootstocks need support.

Pears are grown on quince or pear rootstocks. Pear rootstocks are more tolerant of poorly drained soils than quince. The Quince A is more dwarfing than the Quince C.

STONE FRUIT

Plums are grafted on Myrobalan or St. Julian A rootstocks.

Cherries are grafted on Colt rootstocks which will dwarf the trees by a 1/4 of the standard tree.

Peaches are grown on Siberian C rootstocks

PRUNING

PRUNING AT PLANTING TIME

Although pruning at planting is considered detrimental to the tree, when fruit trees are planted some gardeners restrict the height of the tree by removing the central leader just above the upper most lateral or side branch. Laterals are left until the second year when they are shortened by pruning away half the branch. Cherries, pears and apples are pruned this way. Instead of completely removing the central leader, another method is to prune it back by one third and at the same time reduce the length of the lateral branches by half. This method can also be used for pears, apples and plums.

At planting, raspberries are pruned nine inches (22.5 cm) from the soil line, blackberry canes to ten inches (25 cm).

Gooseberries and red and white currants are pruned so that there are four to five well placed lateral branches. Cut back to the trunk all remaining branches and any suckers that may be growing from the base of the shrub.

Black currants are cut back to within two inches (five cm) of the soil.

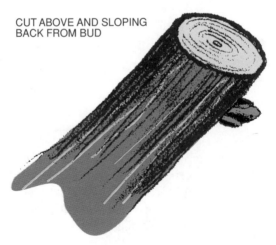

CUT ABOVE AND SLOPING
BACK FROM BUD

When pruning, cut back to just above and sloping back from a bud or shoot that is pointing away from the centre of the tree.

MEDIUM PERENNIALS

• Many perennials are in the easy-to-manage, medium height range. Use them to provide short 3-6 week bursts of seasonal colour.

• Use early flowering perennials to bridge the gap between early bulbs and summer perennials. Similarly, use late-flowering kinds to provide a succession of colour throughout late summer and autumn.

Folse Indigo (Baptisia australis) and Speedwell (Veronica teucrium).

Yellow Loosestrife (Lysimachia punctata), Lulu Lupins and Oriental Poppies.

Plantain Lily (Hosta undulata cultivar) and trunks of European White Birch (Betula pendula).

Purple Cone-flower (Echinacea purpurea) — a medium height perennial.

• Hostas are tough, long-lived, shade tolerant perennials that are well able to compete with the roots of trees and shrubs, making excellent ground covers among such plants. *(above)*

Autumn Stonecrop (Sedum spectabile) — late flowering perennial.

• Many herbaceous perennials will thrive on one application of a complete, balanced fertilizer each year, applied when the new shoots are beginig to show signs of vigorous growth.

• Hoe the fertilizer into the soil surface between plants and "water in" generously.

One of the Sea Hollies (Eryngium spp.) — a long-lived perennial.

Blanbet Flower (Gaillardia aristata) — a cottage garden perennial.

Clustered Bellflower (Campanula glomerata " suberba") — a 1m perennial.

• With perennials, don't put all your eggs in one or two baskets. Don't plant all your early, mid-season or late flowering plants in one spot. Be sure to locate them around the garden so that several clumps of delphiniums, lupins and asters are in bloom throughout the garden at different seasons.

• With perennials, use colours that harmonize or contrast but don't clash. Deep blue and orange is fine, but shocking pink and scarlet may be hard to take.

Golden groundsel (Ligularia "Sungold") - a large, late-flowering perennial.

One of the variegated, ornamental grasses.

LOW PERENNIALS

• When uniformly spaced in groups, many of the more vigorous, mat-forming perennials can be used to create attractive, carpeting ground covers.

Snow-in-summer (Cerastium tomentosum) — a mat-forming perennial.

Carpathian Bell-flower (Campanula carpatica "White Clips") — low perennial.

Japanese Star Primrose (Primula sieboldii) — an early, dwarf perennial.

• Low perennials are a very useful group of plants. Plant them towards the front of the border or in masses to form colourful mats.

• Many mat-forming kinds may be under-planted with early-flowering bulbs. The bulbs emerge first, flowering above the foliage mat, and the perennial flowers later, masking the bulb foliage.

Orange Fleabane (Erigeron aurantiacus) — dwarf perennial — and Wooly Yarrow (Achillea tomentosa).

Alpine Pink (Dianthus alpinus) — a dwarf, mat-forming perennial.

Bloody Cranesbill (Geranium sanguineum) — ground covering perennial.

• Low perennials may also be used as border or bed edgings. As long as not too invasive, they are at home in the rock garden.

• A real advantage to low plants is ease of maintenance. Most don't need staking; they cover the ground, crowding out weeds, and need only a light shearing after flowering to encourage dense foliage growth.

FLOWERING SHRUBS

Purple Smoke Tree (Cotinus coggyria purpureus) — Handsome coloured foliage shrub.

• Several shrubs, including the purple foliaged and flowered Smoke Tree, possess coloured foliage including yellow, purple, silver and variegated. These are valuable sources of long term colour. *(left)*

• While hybrid tea, floribunda and polyantha roses provide flowers throughout the summer, do ask your garden centre about the many shrub roses such as Persian Yellow, Altai, Red-leafed, Hansa and other Japanese Roses. *(right)*

• Consider some of the late summer and fall flowering shrubs including the Snow Hills, Pee Gee and Anabelle Hydrangeas. *(below)*

"Hansa" Rose — An old-fashioned shrub rose.

• Shrubs form a major part of the permanent living structure of the garden. They are particularly useful in providing bursts of colour, especially during spring and early summer—the period during which many of them flower.

• Two valuable groups of long-season, summer flowering shrubs are the small statured, red-flowering bumalda spireas and the 45-120 cm white, yellow, orange, pink and red flowered varieties of shrubby Cinquefoil (*Patentilla fouticosa*).

Snow Hills Hydrangea (Hydrangea arborescens grandiflora) - a late summer-flowering small shrub.

AUTUMN COLOUR

A Dwarf, native willow (Salix spp.) displaying fine autumn tints.

Snowball Tree (Viburnum opulus) — in fruit during winter.

• Several shrubs exhibit brilliant fall colour.

• In garden planning, don't forget to enrich your late season palette by planting a few strategically located plants with outstanding autumn colour. Outstanding plants include Mountain Ash, Peking Cotoneaster, *Euonymus alatus*, Pears, Willows, Birch and several Maples including the outstanding Amur Maple.

Burning Bush (Euonymus alatus) — medium shrub—excellent fall colour.

Pear Trea (Pyrus sp.) in fall colour.

• Don't forget berried plants in your planning. Elders, Bush Honeysuckles, Crabapples, Mountain Ash and Snowball Tree can provide welcome extra late colour with their bright fruits.

FLOWERING TREES

European Mountain Ash (Sorbus aucuparia) — a smaller tree in full fruit.

• Since many urban gardens are not large enough to contain many trees, selecting those that flower makes good sense. In this way, multi-use is achieved. The trees not only provide shade, screening, definition, wind buffering and summer foliage, but a short, spectacular burst of flower colour as well.

• Among outstanding flowering trees are Mountain Ash (also heavily fruited and great autumn colour), Flowering Dogwood, Rosybloom Crabapple, Japanese Tree Lilac, Mayday Tree, Ohio Buckey and Schubert Chokecherry.

Flowering Dogwood (Cornus florida rubra) — a small, early-flowering tree.

Almey Crab-apple, Colorado Blue Spruce and Mayday Tree — a fine spring display.

• Be sure that you have enough room to accommodate the canopy-spread of a tree when it achieves its mature size.

• Flowering trees need to be placed in sunny locations. Too much shade from adjoining trees may inhibit flowering.

Japanese Tree Lilac (Syringa reticulata) — a late-summer-flowering, truly tree-form Lilac.

NON FLOWERING TREES

European White Birch (Betula pendula) — in flower (catkin) in spring.

• While all mature trees produce flowers, many of them are less than conspicuous, such as the catkins of the European Birch and the greenish yellow bracts of the lindens. Since they don't produce what we normally call "flowers," perhaps non-flowering, while not accurate, is appropriate.

• Most non-flowering trees are large shade trees. Great care must be exercised in the placement of large shade trees since they eventually achieve considerable branch spread, resulting in wide-spread shade and lots of invasive roots. Most urban lots are not able to carry more than one to tree such forest giants.

• In urban gardens, trees are best trained and pruned to develop trunks that do not carry any side branches until 1.8-2.4 m above the ground. This results in a higher head or crown which does not take up space at or just above ground level. Thus the land under trees can be used by people or plants.

Amur Maple (Acer ginnala) — a small tree with exquisite autumn colour.

• Larches are an interesting group of conifers. Unlike most needle-lived trees they are deciduous, losing their leaves in the fall like oaks and poplars. In the spring, distinct clusters of needles emerge from dormant buds producing an early flush of brilliant green. The summer foliage is fine-textured and light green, followed by golden autumn tints.

Siberian Larch (Larix sibirica) — a deciduous, cone-bearing tree.

CONIFEROUS EVERGREENS

Atrio of Dwarf Mugho Pines (Pinus mugo pumilio) anchoring a large deck (Canoe Birch trunks).

• Excepting trees and shrubs with coloured bark, evergreens are the only plants which truly provide year-round colour.

• Use coniferous evergreens as accent, foundation and background plants.

• Most of the plants with strong, controlled, architectural forms are in this category. Spruce, fir, Western white cedar and Junipers provide pyramidal, columnar, oval, rounded, spreading and ground-hugging forms.

• Coniferous evergreens provide a wide range of subtle foliage colours ranging from the deep green of mugo pine and Alpine Fir through the yellows, greys, silvers and blues of the junipers to the bright blues of Colorado Spruce varieties.

Branden Columnar Cedar (Thuya occidentalis "Brandon") One of the many column-shaped varieties.

PRUNING GUIDELINES

For general pruning guidelines please refer to the pruning section of Chapter 8, which also applies to fruit trees.

Pruning is used to shape the tree while young and to keep it producing well as it ages. It is important to control the shape and size of the tree to make it attractive and to facilitate maintenance. Pruning opens up the tree, allowing more sun to reach the branches. This increases the amount of fruit and improves its colour. Pruning will help to keep the tree smaller by reducing photosynthesis — the process by which leaves manufacture food that the tree uses to grow. Trees that are pruned will have stouter trunks than those left unpruned. Pruning is invigorating and will stimulate strong new growth. The tree should be lightly pruned annually rather than letting it get out of hand and removing a lot of wood at one time. If a tree is heavily pruned, undesirable vigorous upright shoots (water shoots) will grow along the branches.

Generally, cut back to just above and sloping back from a bud or shoot that is pointing outward — away from the centre of the tree.

FRUIT TREES

Fruit trees are pruned in Vancouver during the dormant season, usually from mid-December through mid-February.

Apples and pears are borne on spurs (short, slow growing branches that produce fruiting buds), arising from two or more year old wood. Up to 10% of the old fruiting branches could be pruned away each year.

Peaches fruit on two year old wood (the previous season's growth). Remove the shoots that bore fruit, after harvesting, to make room for new fruiting shoots. You can remove 20 per cent of the old wood each year.

Plums are borne on spurs which should be kept shortened. At maturity, renew one third of the fruiting wood each year by removing side shoots — lateral branches which develop from the main branch — back to the branch, causing new growth to form.

Sweet cherries are produced on wood that is two or more years old. Sour cherries are produced on last year's wood and an ongoing renewal is necessary.

Summer pruning is practiced particularly on espalier fruit trees. It involves removing some of the new growth at the beginning of July, and then again at the beginning of August if there is a lot of new growth. Removing leaves reduces plant food production, helping reduce the vigour of the tree, keeping it smaller and reducing the amount of winter pruning that will need to be done. The first week in July, each current shoot is cut back, leaving three leaves. The process is repeated again the first week in August, when you cut back to the first leaf of the newest flush of growth. The shoots are not pruned unless they have reached 9 to 12 inches (22.5 to 30 cm) in length and the stem is as thick as a pencil.

PRUNING IN YEARS TO COME

If the central leader was removed at planting time in the second winter, all the rest of the branches are shortened by half. Keep about four well spaced branches with wide crotches and remove any other branches. In the third winter there will be new shoots on those branches. Again select strong, well placed shoots and prune away any that are misplaced. The shoots that were retained should be reduced by half. The tree will have a nice framework of branches. In subsequent winters, pruning will consist of removing or shortening any branches that cross over on the inside of the tree.

If the central leader was retained at planting, pruning the following winter will consist of shortening all the previous season's growth by one third. Completely remove from the top any previous season's growth that is upright and could form another leader. In each subsequent year the leader is shortened. It is important for the tree to have wide angled side branches. In the second summer, if necessary, a wooden spacer such as a stick is wedged in the crotch of the branch and the trunk to force the branch down, increasing the angle. A wider angled branch is less susceptible to breakage.

Cane Fruit   Canes that have borne fruit are removed either in the summer or in the fall right down to within an inch or so of the ground. If there has been a disease or insect problem, remove the old canes immediately after harvest.

Bush Fruit   Blueberries are pruned during the dormant season. Weak growth and some older wood is removed.

Black currants are borne on the previous year's wood. When harvesting, the whole branch may be removed as it will not bear fruit again.

Gooseberries and red and white currants are trained to produce one, two and three year old shoot systems. Each year remove the older systems. Tip growth can also be pruned back by one third at the end of June.

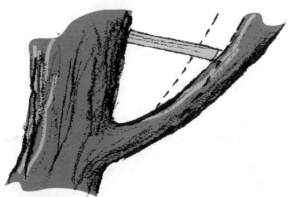

It is important for a tree to have wide angled side branches, because they are less susceptible to breakage. A stick wedged in the crotch of the branch and the trunk will force the branch down and increase the angle.

DEBLOSSOMING

Fruit trees should not be allowed to bear fruit until they are three years old. Remove blossoms to prevent fruit set and direct the tree's energies into wood production.

JUNE DROP

Fruit drop is very frustrating to the gardener. It looks like your whole crop is landing on the ground; however, it is normal for a certain amount of fruit to drop in June. There are often two drops, one earlier in the month and one later. The small fruit may not have been pollinated and would never develop. The tree will also drop excess fruit in years when it has set a heavy crop. Stress, excess moisture, drought or pests and diseases will also cause fruit to drop prematurely.

FRUIT THINNING

If the fruit on your trees or grape vines is very heavy, it should be thinned after the June drop. There should be a space as wide as your hand between the centers of each developing fruit.

WATERING

Vancouver usually has plenty of water, except during the summer. Even then, some years provide a fair amount of rain. Newly planted trees and shrubs need to be watered during the first few years, especially during dry periods. Larger trees will need additional water in dry summers.

FERTILIZING

All fruits should be fertilized in the spring. Use a basic fertilizer like 6-8-6. Fertilizer late in the season will prevent the plants from the hardening off which can lead to winter damage.

PEST CONTROL

Weeds must be kept under control particularly when the trees are young. Once mature, a ground cover like grass may be grown under them.

Powdery mildew is a prevalent disease which can infect most plants. It can be reduced by increasing air circulation.

Do not crowd plants, and judiciously remove excess branches.

Peaches can be infected with peach leaf curl. In the winter when the plants are dormant, spray them with dormant oil, alone or mixed with sulfur, to eradicate the disease. Where possible, plant the trees under the overhang of the roof to keep the rain off.

Pear trellis rust is controlled by removing infected junipers, the alternate host of the disease. Apple or pear scab is prevalent. Grow resistant varieties like Bartlett pears and King, Spartan and Transparent apples.

Black knot is prevalent on plums and needs to be pruned out in March. Prune back three to four inches (7.5-10 cm) beyond the point of damage into sound, healthy wood.

Insect pests can include a variety of caterpillars, which should be picked off.

Gooseberries and currants are often infested by fruit fly larvae. Keep diseased fruit picked off the plants and ground. The next year spray with malathion late in the evening ten days after blossoming starts and repeat it twice more at weekly intervals.

There are many other pests that can be a problem at various times. Consult the Pest Prevention and Control booklet published by the BC Ministry of Agriculture and Fisheries or phone the hortline at UBC or VanDusen Botanic Garden for help.

POOR FRUIT SET

Fruit set can be poor due to weather. A late frost can kill buds and flowers. If the weather is very wet, bees that pollinate the fruit may not be flying. Some fruit trees naturally bear heavily one year and lightly the next. Insect pests and disease, as well as other stressful conditions, like poor nutrition or lack of water when the fruit buds are developing the previous summer, can affect fruiting.

HARVESTING AND STORAGE

Knowing the correct time for harvesting comes with experience but the very best test is the taste test! Storage differs from fruit to fruit. Small fruits, for the most part, freeze well or can be made into preserves. Apples are stored at just above freezing temperature. Most fruits will keep a week or so in the refrigerator.

UNUSUAL FRUIT TO GROW IN VANCOUVER

QUINCE

The quince is an attractive tree that produces woolly yellow fruit, harvested in late fall. A pome fruit, it has been grown in Europe since early times. The fruit is not eaten out of hand, but makes wonderful jam. Quince trees are not large, growing to about 12 feet (3.6 m), and can be espaliered against a fence or wall. Grow them in a sunny spot in deep loam. The only pest problem seems to be pear slugs, which can be controlled by removing the affected leaves.

FIG

The fig will grow in Vancouver in a sheltered spot against a building, in full sun. There are several fine old trees in Vancouver. They can also be espaliered. On the coast, they usually produce one crop each year. In harsh winters they may die back but grow quickly. Mulch them heavily in the fall. Two fig varieties are Brown Turkey and King.

MEDLAR

Medlars are rarely grown now, but form attractive trees that can be espaliered. There is a nice example at Cecil Green Park on the UBC campus. Because medlar fruit is very hard, it must be left until rotted or bletted (softened) before eaten. It then has the texture of soft apple sauce and a not unpleasant taste.

NUTS

Some nut trees to try growing in Vancouver are hazelnuts (still grown commercially in the Fraser Valley), Carpathian walnuts, chestnuts and filberts. Nut tree yields can be variable, and some years there are very few nuts to harvest.

WOODY ORNAMENTALS

THE DIFFERENT FORMS

There are five basic forms in which a deciduous tree can be trained: standard, half-standard, low-headed, multi-stemmed and bush. The standard form has a single, straight trunk which is free of branches to a height of six feet (1.8 m). A half-standard tree is similar but has a branch-free trunk to a height of only three to four feet (0.9 to 1.2 m). Low-headed trees have short trunks, often less than three feet (0.9 m) high. A multi-stemmed tree is a high, medium, or occasionally low-headed tree with more than one main trunk. The ideal multi-stemmed form has three equally spaced trunks of equal girth and height. More than five trunks tend to make a tree look like a large shrub.The bush form has several main stems originating at or near ground level, forming a large, shrub-like plant.

Shrubs can be defined as woody plants, generally of smaller stature than trees, with several main shoots originating at or near ground level. A shrub is usually well branched and carries foliage from top to bottom.

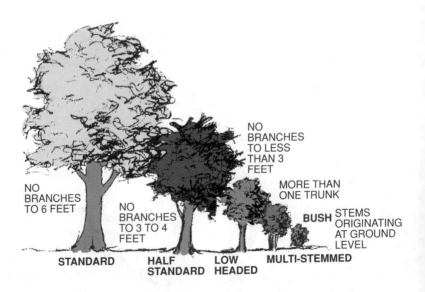

The five basic forms in which a deciduous tree can be trained.

The distinction between a large shrub and a small "bush-form" tree is a bit blurred and arbitrary. Size is the major distinguishing characteristic.

Vines are climbing or trailing plants. Perennial kinds usually have woody stems while annuals are soft and fleshy.

Ground covers are low growing, woody and herbaceous perennial plants used to cover the soil surface of an area.

LOCATION AND PLACEMENT

Chapter 2, Garden Planning, discusses the placement of trees and shrubs in the garden.

There is a lot to consider when planting trees and shrubs, particularly in a city lot. Trees in Vancouver are always an emotional issue. The city has made laws about removing trees, so your original choice is important. The ultimate height and the amount of space a tree will need is critical. The full-grown tree should not dwarf the house, and chestnuts, big-leaf maples, and the fascinating monkey puzzle tree may be more at home in a park than your yard. The same consideration applies to shrubs, especially larger kinds. Nothing is more irritating than bumping into the branches of a shrub that has grown too large for its space along the sidewalk.

If there are overhead wires along your street, plant the trees far enough away so they will not interfere. When the crews come along and cut the trees back they just shear off the offending branches, leaving a badly misshapen tree.

Although trees create shade, they need sun to do well, particularly flowering trees. It is difficult to grow most perennials and annuals in a yard that is too shady. You might appreciate the shade of a large tree in the summer but not in the winter, so your choice of trees might be deciduous rather than evergreen. An evergreen tree planted in front of a window can make a room too dark.

Plant winter flowering shrubs where they can be enjoyed from a window or along a walkway rather than across the lawn. Fragrant plants should also be placed where you can easily enjoy their scent.

Flowering shrubs need to be planted where their flowers will complement surrounding plants. Deciduous azaleas in particular have flowers in almost neon shades and need to be handled with care.

SIZE AND FORM AT MATURITY

In order to plan the placement and effect of trees and shrubs in a garden, it is necessary to know three things—the height, spread and form of the plants when they reach maturity. This data makes it possible to decide which trees and shrubs can be planted and where, how far apart they should be planted to create a specific landscape effect, what will be the predictable future effects of size, shade and root spread on the garden, and what will be the aesthetic effect of the plants on the garden landscape.

DEFINING MATURE SIZE

Defining the size of a tree or shrub at maturity is difficult, since each plant grows differently, and soils and gardening techniques vary. A reasonable definition is the approximate size of a nursery grown and formed tree, 25 to 30 years after planting in an urban garden where it received regular watering and good garden care. In the case of a shrub, size at maturity may be defined as the approximate size achieved under a regimen of regular watering and good garden care before old age and/or poor form suggest rejuvenation pruning or replacement.

Major long range landscape problems that stem from inadequate knowledge about size at maturity include planting where there is insufficient space for a plant to mature and produce the garden designer's intended effect; planting trees and shrubs too close together to allow each to exhibit its true from; planting too close to houses, walls, fences, pathways, driveways, and neighbours, blocking access, vision and light; and the need for unnecessary pruning to keep rampant growers and overgrown plants in reasonable bounds.

The key to preventing such problems is knowing and taking into account the height, spread and form of trees and shrubs at maturity before planting.

SUITABILITY

When buying plants, consider whether they are prone to disease or insects. In Vancouver, junipers are the alternate host to Pear Trellis Rust. Choose a different plant like Russian Cypress to achieve a similar effect. Instead of growing native dogwood, which is susceptible to anthracnose, plant *Cornus kousa*, the Japanese dogwood, which is resistant to the disease.

Consider native plants: *Vaccinium ovatum* 'Thunderbird,' a new UBC Plant introduction, *Mahonias*, salal *(Gaultheria shallon)*, the native red currant *(Ribes sanguinium)* or its white form 'White Icicle.' Native plants are often overlooked in favour of exotic plants from other countries, but many are very ornamental.

Consider aspect. Most plants do not bloom well in deep shade. Even shade-loving rhododendrons need some sun to bloom well. Plants that have good fall colour need the sun. The wonderful red fall colour of *Euonymous alatus* is not as intense on the shady side of the hedge surrounding the Contemporary Garden at UBC.

Some plants have bad habits that should be considered. Walnuts should not be planted near the vegetable or flower garden. Their roots give off a chemical that keeps other plants from growing. They also compete for nutrients. *Rhus typhina* can produce a lot of suckers and some trees can produce a lot of unwanted fruit. Other plants have poisonous berries or fruit which should be considered if there are young children. The *Laburnum* and *Daphne laureola* are two examples.

HARDINESS

In Vancouver, we have the warmest climate in Canada and are able to grow plants that will not grow anywhere else in the nation. However, that does not mean that everything will grow here. A tree or shrub that is hardy in Vancouver will survive our coldest winters and grow where there is lots of rain and little summer heat. Even so, we often take chances and grow plants that are borderline hardy, like the beautiful Hebes. Every six or seven years we get a bad winter and they are killed. Sometimes we find a sheltered place possessing a warmer micro-climate which is the perfect spot to grow a plant that may be tender. Plants can be protected from the cold by mulching them in the fall and wrapping the trunk or branches of evergreen plants with burlap.

YEAR ROUND INTEREST

Find out how a plant looks throughout the year. Does it have good fall colour, when does it bloom, does it have interesting fruit, do the leaves have an interesting texture, is it evergreen or deciduous? In Vancouver, our biggest flush of colour from trees and shrubs is in the spring: ornamental cherries and plums, azaleas and rhododendrons, camelias and a hundred other spring flowering plants.

> **It is always more difficult to find plants that bloom later. Some to consider include *Davidia involucrata*, the Dove Tree, *Stewaria* species with their camelia-like flowers, and the summer flowering hydrangeas. Look for some of the more unusual hydrangeas rather than the commonly seen blue varieties.**

Vines are a great addition to a garden. Depending on the species, you can have bloom from the early spring through fall. Grow them up into trees, along fences, up walls or tumbling over shrubs, banks and walls. They are very versatile and add another dimension to the garden. Some vines that are great for Vancouver are *Akebia quinata, Campsis radicans, Actinidia, Clematis, Hydrangea petiolaris, Schizophragma* and *Wisteria*, as well as the more commonly seen ivies, to name a few.

Conifers, with their shades of green, can be a wonderful backdrop or foil for other plants or can be a focal point. There are many shapes and sizes to choose from, both native and exotic, including clones that are grown for their unusual growth habits, texture or colour.

Fall colour is not restricted to maples but is provided by vines like *Vitis* and trees like *Sorbus, Rhus typhina, Parrotia persica, Liquidambar*, and so many more.

Interest in the garden doesn't need to end in the fall. Many plants provide winter colour. Vancouver is blessed with many plants that bloom in the winter, from the low growing hellebores, *Jasminum nudiflorum* and

Sarcococca to shrubs like *Rhododendron mucronulatum, Chimonanthus praecox, Hamamelis mollis* and *Cornus mas*, the Cornelian cherry. Many shrubs have buds that are interesting in winter and then bloom early in the spring like *Garrya eliptica, Corylopsis sinensis*, and *Stachyurus chinensis*.

There are trees and shrubs that produce wonderful berries, from the more common pyracanthas and cotoneasters to the fascinating purple berries of the *Callicarpa bodinieri*, the pink berries of *Sorbus hupehensis* 'Pink Pagoda' or the vivid red berries of *Skimmia japonica*.

It is hard to stop here because we are so fortunate to be able to grow such interesting plants. Palms, bamboos, magnolias, hardy fucshias, ferns and fremontodendrons — the list is almost never ending, including plants with interesting bark and wonderfully coloured spring growth.

PLANTS FOR SPECIAL PLACES

Even though we are blessed with lots of rain there is sometimes a need for plants that will withstand drought, either under an overhang or in the rain shadow of a building. Consider planting *Acuba japonica, Mahonia, Ginkgo, Arbutus unedo* or the Japanese Holly *(Ilex crenata)*.

If the soil is poorly drained, some plants that tolerate "wet feet" are *Metasequoia* 'Dawn Redwood'; *Pernettya mucronata; Ilex aquifolium* 'European Holly'; *Rosa rugosa* 'saltspray rose'; *Gaultheria shallon* 'Salal'; and *Cercidiphyllum*, the Katsura tree.

If a ground cover is wanted, consider *Genista pilosa 'Vancouver Gold'* — a wonderful ground hugging broom, *Rubus calycinoides*, cotoneasters and ivies.

If you have a pond or pool in your yard, carefully choose nearby trees and shrubs. A swimming pool needs to be kept free of debris. Trees such as willows may look lovely hanging over a large pond, but leaf and twig drop is a nuisance.

SOIL PREPARATION

Soil preparation is discussed in Chapter 3. Trees and shrubs will benefit from organic matter dug into the top soil. Make sure some of the mulch is mixed with the soil along the sides of the hole to make it less of a transition for the roots as they grow into the existing soil. Do not leave the sides of the hole slick, smooth or glazed as they can become a barrier that roots cannot penetrate. This can happen when the hole is dug by machine or if the soil is mostly wet clay.

Trees and shrubs will not need to be fertilized in the first year, but they can be fed in subsequent years in the spring using a basic fertilizer such as 6-8-6. Every three or four years top dress the soil with compost.

MULCHING

Trees and shrubs benefit from a layer of mulch — no thicker than four inches (10 cm). Any well rotted compost, mushroom manure or leaf mold will work well. Never use fresh manure or compost because it will kill tender roots.

PURCHASING PLANTS

Chapter 7, the fruit chapter, explains what to look for when buying trees or shrubs and how to care for them. Generally, trees and shrubs are not available bare rooted in Vancouver but are balled and burlapped or in containers. Never buy a plant unless it looks healthy, with no sign of disease or pests. Do not pick the biggest or the smallest plant. Choose one that has sturdy branches, pleasingly placed. The bark should not have any gouges in it or marks that might indicate disease or insect damage. There should not be a lot of roots coming out the bottom of the pot, which might indicate the plant is root bound. It should be correctly labelled. Buy from nurseries that are neat and tidy, indicating that they have pride in their professionalism. It also means that pests are less likely to be a problem when debris is absent. The nursery should have knowledgeable staff who know the plants they sell. Buy locally-grown plants wherever possible. They will be physiologically hardier during the first winter than the same cultivar grown in California and shipped to Vancouver.

PLANTING TREES AND SHRUBS

When planting in unimproved soil, the hole should be at least nine inches (22.5 cm) wider than the root ball. If the soil is being amended, the hole should be twice the diameter of the root ball. The plant should be sitting slightly higher than the surrounding, undisturbed soil to allow for the soil settling. It is important ultimately to not have the soil-root ball covered by more than a one inch (2.5 cm) depth of new soil. If the roots are very compacted, gently tease the outer roots, slightly pulling them away from the root ball. Any broken roots should be trimmed neatly. If the roots are circling the container they should be straightened out. Cut through if this is not possible.

Completely remove metal and plastic containers. With compressed fibre pots, remove as much of the container as possible. Often, the container can be slit down the sides and removed. Burlap and other balling materials should be cut away. When positioning the root ball in the planting hole, treat it with care. Do not allow it to break apart.

Back-fill with soil, tamping it lightly to eliminate air pockets. A ring of soil can be placed, forming a dish around the root zone of the newly planted tree or shrub. This will help to hold the water that first season when it is so important for the plant to get enough moisture.

To stake or not to stake? Generally in the home garden it isn't necessary unless the site is very windy, the root ball is too small or, in the case of apple trees like the M9, the rootstocks are brittle. Trees develop better trunks if they are able to move rather than being held rigid by a stake. Shrubs should not need to be staked.

Vines will need a stake to climb on until they reach the surface they are to cover. Plant vines a yard away from the trunk when they are to be trained up a tree.

TRANSPLANTING

The best time to move established trees or shrubs within the garden is the fall. With our mild winter, plants have a chance to re-establish their root system when it is cool and the plants are dormant. Valuable large trees can be moved by professional tree movers. Plants can also be moved throughout the winter as long as the ground isn't frozen. The spring is also a good time for transplanting. If a plant must be moved in the summer, give it some shade if possible and enough water to reduce the shock. Make-shift shade can be supplied using cardboard, an old sheet between stakes or even a patio umbrella stuck in the ground. It is important to minimize stress wherever possible and to give the plant adequate water for the first year while the roots are re-establishing themselves.

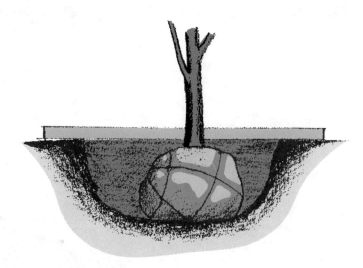

When planting a tree or shrub, burlap and other balling material should be cut away. It is important not to have the root ball covered by more than a one inch depth of new soil.

GENERAL GUIDELINES

If trees and shrubs are carefully chosen, very little pruning will be necessary. Choose plants that will not outgrow their allotted spaces. Then in future years only a bit of tidying up pruning will be needed, or perhaps some renewal pruning in the case of some shrubs.

Plants are pruned to enhance their appearance and keep them healthy by removing diseased or insect infested wood. The careful removal of branches can allow more sun into the garden as well as into the centre of the tree. Pruning can sometimes give new life to a tree that seems to be just sitting there. With a little help from the gardener the tree can develop well spaced branches and be a pleasure to look at.

Pruning is a difficult subject to talk about as we grow so many different types of trees and shrubs in Vancouver. It is very hard to generalize, since each individual plant is unique, but here are some general guidelines.

PRUNING AT PLANTING TIME

Pruning at planting time is now thought to be detrimental to the plant. Unless there are broken branches to be removed, it will not need pruning.

Before you put the pruners to any plant, stand back and have a good look at it. What shape does it naturally have? Plants should be pruned to enhance this shape. Forsythias are shrubs with naturally arching branches. They look unnatural when pruned into a ball. Trees that are naturally upright cannot easily be forced into a spreading habit. Shrubs that have become too large for the site should be removed to a better spot rather than drastically pruning them back all the time.

TREES

Many deciduous trees such as *Acer palmatum*, *A. japonicum*, *Cornus kousa* and magnolias will need very little pruning.

If large trees have outgrown their space or have large branches that need to be removed, this is usually a job for a professional tree pruner. Although conifers look better if they are left unpruned, the lower limbs can be removed to open up the area beneath for growing other plants. If the garden is very shady, judiciously remove some of the conifer's branches here and there throughout its length to allow more light through.

The first step in pruning is to remove any broken, weak, damaged or diseased branches back to their point of origin. Then remove branches that are crossing through the center of the tree. Make the pruning cut flush with the basal collar without leaving a jagged edge. The basal collar or branch is the wrinkled bark area where the branch joins the trunk. The collar helps to heal the wound.

Before removing anything else step back and have another look to see how the branches that have been removed affect the overall shape. It is better to stop too soon than too late. Once the branch is removed it can't be glued back on.

Remove over-crowded branches, those that are rubbing against each other or that detract from the overall shape. If a branch has a narrow crotch (see the diagram in the fruit chapter) it should be removed because it will be weak. If the tree is young and the branch is well placed, a stick could be used to exert pressure to widen the crotch.

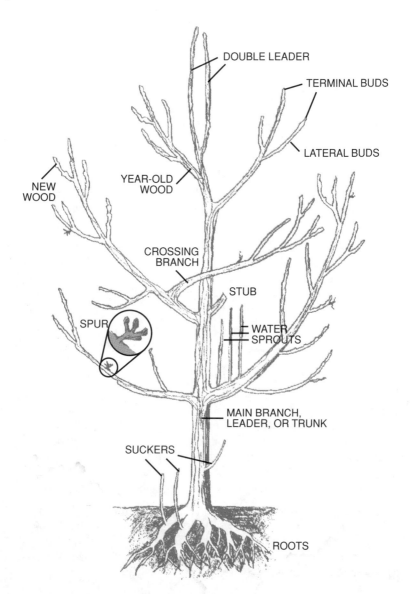

When pruning has been heavy the previous season the tree responds by sending out strong whippy growth, called water sprouts, often along the mature limbs. Prune these right back to their origin.

If there is more than one strong shoot at the top of the tree, all but one should be removed. Only one central leader is wanted.

Once they have matured, most trees will grow without much pruning, other than to tidy them up. If a plant needs drastic pruning to keep it in bounds, you have planted it in the wrong place.

The second step is to shorten the existing branches if that is desired, as in the case of roses. Make the cut one quarter inch (0.6 cm) past a bud that is facing towards the outside of the branch. This dormant bud will grow into a new branch and it will grow in the direction the bud is facing.

It is hard on a plant when it is drastically pruned, and the plant responds by producing an excess of new growth. Instead, prune the plant a little each year.

SHRUBS

Deciduous shrubs that grow slowly, such as *Corylopsis*, *Daphne*, *Euonymus*, *Hamamelis*, *Hibiscus syriacus* and *Fothergilla*, will require very little pruning. Spring flowering shrubs such as *Deutzia*, *Forsythia*, *Kerria*, *Weigela* and *Ribes sanguineum*, that bloom on the previous season's growth, are pruned back immediately after flowering. Cut the branches that have flowered back down to where new growth is coming out on the main stems. Each year, prune out at ground level one quarter of the oldest or weakest stems.

Spent *Hydrangea* blossoms should be left on the shrub until late winter before they are removed to a strong set of buds. The old flowers will help to protect the flower buds during cold spells.

Deciduous shrubs that bloom on current season's growth, like *Buddleia davidii*, *Romneya* and *Hydrangea paniculata*, can be cut back in March to within a couple of buds on last season's growth. *Cotinus* may also be treated this way if you want to keep it small and enjoy its new foliage each year, although it will not bloom.

Roses are pruned from mid-February to mid-March. The same general pruning rules apply. Remove dead, diseased, crossing over branches and any weak growth first. Reduce the remaining vigourous stems back to 10 inches (25 cm) and to an outward facing bud.

In October, prune back the roses by one third to remove the dead flowers and the newest weaker growth. By waiting until spring to do the major pruning there is less chance of the plants being winter killed.

During the growing season, prune spent flowers.

Climbing roses bloom on shoots that arise on the previous year's growth. In the late summer, prune all the shoots along the main stems to within two buds or eyes. Cut back one or two of the oldest main canes to within 18 inches (45 cm) of the ground to encourage strong replacement growth.

Evergreen shrubs are mostly left unpruned except for a bit of cosmetic touching up. Spent blooms can be removed, as with lavenders, but usually they crop without intervention.

> **As a general rule of thumb, spring-flowering shrubs are pruned immediately after they have bloomed.**

A lot of evergreen shrubs, like rhododendrons and azaleas, need very little pruning except to remove a wayward branch.

Covering the pruning cut with pruning paste is not generally done now. It has been shown that the tree will heal better on its own.

Conifers, like pines, that form candles of new growth at the end of the previous season's shoots, can be pruned by removing one third of the new growth in the spring. It can easily be pinched off with the fingers. Conifers are not generally pruned unless grown as hedges. Then they are pruned in July. Once the hedge has reached the desired height, remove the leaders or top growth.

To lighten up a dense conifer, whole branches can be removed here and there up the length of the tree. If this is carefully done the shape of the tree isn't destroyed, yet more light will filter through.

Espaliering, pollarding and pleaching are different ways to prune trees and shrubs with varying results. Espaliering is the training method which can be used for fruit trees predominantly. It is an art which requires pruning knowledge and the resulting patterns can take many years to complete. Pollarding, cutting all the branches back to the trunk each year, is seen more often in Europe. In the spring a profusion of whippy growth results. The results are awful. Why anyone would treat a tree this way is beyond me.

Pleaching was done in some of the old European gardens where the branches of a row of trees were twined together, forming a thick hedge or tunnel. It is seldom seen, except in old estate gardens.

WHERE TO BUY PLANTS

Vancouver has a climate suitable for so many different plants that we should try to grow some of the more uncommon kinds rather than planting the same plants seen growing in everyone else's garden. There are nurseries that grow unusual trees and shrubs and good local plant stores will try to track down unusual plants for you. Check out the gardens in Vancouver, both private and public, for ideas of interesting looking plants. Although the UBC Botanical garden sells predominantly interesting perennials, they often have some choice trees and shrubs. These are small plants that have been propagated by the volunteers.

DAMAGE TO TREES

Sometimes trees begin to look unwell and it is difficult to figure out why.

Was the past winter very severe? Sometimes a plant looks like it has survived and may even have bloomed only to die in the summer. The winter damage to the root system was too severe.

Has there been any new construction near the tree in the last five years or so? It may take a large tree or shrub several seasons to show the damage that was done to its roots.

Have you altered the site? Raising the soil level or building a patio over the roots can kill a tree. Roots must have air to live and most of the tree's roots are near the surface and go well beyond the drip line (an imaginary line drawn on the ground below the tree at the point to which the outermost branch extends).

Altering the site may affect the drainage and some trees are very susceptible to root rot, particularly cedars.

Did the plants get adequate water the previous summer? Sometimes we can have several months with no rain, which is very hard on shallow rooted trees and shrubs.

> **Check plants for insects or diseases. One borer can kill a small tree and the only evidence is one small hole on the trunk.**
>
> **Check the trunk for damage. Did it get bashed by the lawn mower or weed eater, or did a rodent dine on the bark during the winter? If the trunk is completely ringed, nutrients are unable to move up the tree.**

CHAPTER 9

LAWNS

Lawns are communities of grass plants, growing closely together with each plant actively competing for space, nutrients and water and capable of living for a hundred years. This suggests that lawns should be constructed with considerable care. There is only one opportunity to do the job properly — the first time. Once the lawn has been sown or sodded, there is really nothing that can be done to improve inadequate soil preparation, short of reconstruction.

Once the lawn is growing, a first class, regular maintenance program is necessary to ensure the longevity, good health, vigour and beauty of the lawn.

CONSTRUCTION

DRAINAGE

The area which is going to be lawn must be well drained. Water must not stand in pools on the surface for more than a few hours after a heavy rain. Additional information about drainage can be found in Chapter 3.

WEED CONTROL

Prior to grading or soil preparation it is important to eliminate all weeds from the area. If there are only a few annual weeds, they can be pulled by hand or hoed out, but if the area is heavily infested, particularly with perennial weeds, a weed killer may be necessary.

A broad spectrum herbicide should be used that will kill both grasses and broad leafed weeds. Herbicides containing the chemical glyphosate will kill most weeds with the exception of perennial morning glory and horsetails.

The herbicide should be applied according to the manufacturer's instructions on the container.

> **The weeds must be actively growing to achieve the best results. Caution should be used because this type of herbicide is not selective. It must not be allowed to drift onto other plants. Spray only on a calm day and apply it using a low pressure, large droplet spray. The coverage should be even and thorough for best results.**

If you must spray near established beds, use a large board or piece of cardboard as a barrier between the spray and the plants. If in doubt, wash off the plants with clean water.

Do not step in the solution and walk on the lawn. Remember that just a touch on a green shoot or leaf can move through the plant and kill it. Yet once glyphosate touches the soil it becomes inactive, which means that once the weeds have died it is safe to sow grass seed or put down sod. It does not kill the weeds instantly and must be allowed time to kill the root. Once the leaves have turned brown, which may take several weeks, the soil can be cultivated.

GRADING

It is important to develop a uniform depth of top soil overlying a reasonably uniform depth of subsoil in order to construct a lawn of even texture and colour.

If a reasonably level or gently rolling lawn is desired but the site is undulating, it may be necessary to:
- move the top soil to one side of the site, just off the area to be constructed.
- grade and contour the subsoil to follow the final surface grades and contours, allowing for the replacement of top soil to final levels.
- apply a two inch (five cm) deep layer of peatmoss over the subsoil and work it in thoroughly, 9 to 12 inches (22.5 to 30 cm) deep.
- re-spread the top soil to final surface contours and grades.

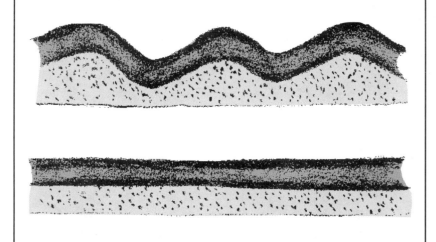

Slopes Except for larger scale, contoured lawns, construct slopes at less than 15 per cent or 15 feet (4.5 m) vertical over 100 feet (30 m) horizontal.

The maximum safely mowable slope is one foot (30 cm), vertical, over three feet (90 cm) horizontal.

Minimum slopes to ensure adequate surface drainage are:

- 1% or one foot (30 cm) in 100 feet (30 m) on well drained sites,and
- 2% or two feet (60 cm) in 100 feet (30 m) on poorly drained sites.

Terraces Terraced lawns are an excellent way to develop sloping land. They add strong visual interest to the landscape, increase the functionality of the garden and provide definition and enclosure to garden spaces. Whenever possible be sure to exploit differences in elevation by terracing.

Matching Elevations Where lawns are planned to abut pathways and other paved areas, leave the final compacted soil level 1/4-1 inch (0.6-2.5 cm) above the hard surface so that, after settling, the lawn will be at or a little above the elevation of the hard surface. Few sights in a garden look more untidy than ragged grass edges, growing above or below a paved area.

SOIL PREPARATION

General considerations and methods are discussed in Chapter 3. However, when constructing lawns, top soil preparation should be carried out with considerable care. If a long lived, healthy, vigorous, dense, nice textured, deep green, self-healing lawn is desired, a minimum depth of six inches (15 cm), [preferably nine inches (22.5 cm)] of well prepared top soil is required. For sodded lawns this depth includes the thickness of the sod.

Specific preparation methods are:

- use moist, granular, sphagnum peat moss as the source of organic matter. Apply a one inch (2.5 cm) layer over the soil surface for each four inch (10 cm) depth of top soil to be cultivated. Do not exceed this amount, or a spongy, rather than resilient lawn will result.
- apply 22 lbs. (10 kg) of 10-20-10 fertilizer per 1076 sq.ft. (100 m^2) of lawn.
- thoroughly mix the peat and fertilizer with the top soil.
- the soil in Vancouver tends to be acidic. Grass grows best when the pH is 6.5 (slightly acidic). If the soil tests less than 6.0, lime should be added. It takes 66 lbs. (30 kg) of lime per 1076 sq.ft. (100 m^2) of soil area to raise the pH from 5 to 6.5. Spread the lime evenly over the soil surface.

- consolidate the top soil by heeling - that's an old Scottish green-keepers' technique of walking over the land in closely spaced rows on the heels with your toes turned up. Remember that freshly dug soil will settle about 20 per cent of its height.

SEED BED PREPARATION

Using a good quality steel rake, rake and cross-rake the area to develop a uniform, 1.5 to 2 inch (3.75 to 5 cm) deep layer of fine, granular soil particles. Remember, the job is not complete until you have achieved the final, finished lawn surface grade. Also bear in mind that you only get one chance to do it right — the first time. Short of re-seeding or re-sodding, there's little that can be done to correct unsatisfactory surface grades after the grass is established.

SEED SOWING

Most seed mixtures are sown at a rate of 4 lbs.(1.8 kg) per 1000 sq.ft. (93 m^2) of lawn area.

It is of paramount importance to sow evenly and uniformly. When hand sowing this is more easily achieved by:
- mixing the seed with three to five times its bulk of sand, vermiculite, perlite or fine, dry soil as a spreader. It's much easier to spread the larger volume evenly over the same size area.
- sowing half the seed over the entire area in a north-south direction and the other half in an east-west direction.

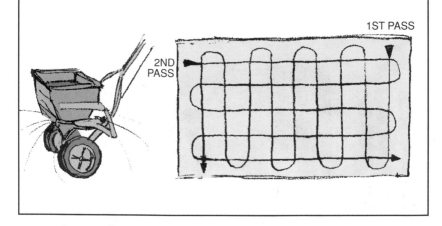

There is also a wide range of mechanical spreaders available for purchase or rent. The rotary plate type spreads very evenly and is easy to use. A hand held model is adequate for seeding and fertilizing in the average urban garden.

After sowing, rake over the area gently and shallowly in one direction only. It's a mistake to bury the seed too deeply.

To shade the soil surface from direct sun and excessive drying and encourage quick sprouting, a little chopped straw may be scattered over the surface, but this is not mandatory. It may be left on to be chopped up by the mower after the grass is well established.

WATERING

The general rule is to water copiously when water is needed, leaving as long as practical between waterings. This encourages deep rooting and promotes drought resistance.

However, this rule does not apply when watering a newly-seeded lawn. Prior to seed sprouting, watering must be frequent and light, using a fine spray. Avoid puddling and eroding the soil surface. The aim is to maintain the soil surface in a uniformly moist but not soggy condition, to promote maximum and even seed germination.

After germination, when the young grass plants are well rooted, watering frequency and volume can be increased, gradually reinstating the general rule.

FIRST CUT

As soon as the new grass is about four inches (10 cm) high, it may be topped by cutting to three inches (7.5 cm). During subsequent cuts, lower the height of cut by 1/2 inch (1.25 cm) per cut, until the regular cutting height of one to two inches (2.5-5 cm) is reached.

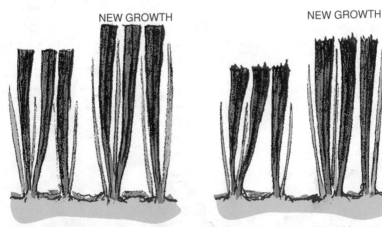

NEW GROWTH   NEW GROWTH

It is important to maintain a sharp mower. Sharp cuts heal cleanly and quickly, promoting fast growth, while ragged cuts result in slow healing and recovery.

TYPES OF GRASSES

A good lawn seed mixture for an average lawn contains, by weight, 30 per cent Kentucky bluegrass, 50 per cent fine fescue, which includes slender creeping and red creeping, and 20 per cent perennial rye. It is seeded at a rate of 1.8 kg/100 m² (4 lbs./1076 sq.ft.). If the area has moderate shade, use 20 per centrough bluegrass and 40 per cent fine fescues and 40 per cent perennial rye because the fescues are more shade tolerant than the bluegrass. Sow 2 kg/100 m² (4.4 lbs./1076 sq.ft.).

If your lawn area is deeply shaded, it will quickly become invaded with moss. Moss killers will kill the moss, but unless the shade is reduced it will come back. Lime does not kill moss but makes the growing conditions less inviting. In shady places, ground covers are more practical than grass. Consider planting Hostas, ivy, or *Pachysandra*.

In most years, during July and August we have very little rain and the grass will turn brown unless watered. Many areas have water restrictions during the summer. As we become more conscious of water usage it is becoming acceptable to allow the lawn to go dormant over the summer. It will turn brown, but do not worry. It will quickly green up with the first rains in the fall.

SODDING OR TURFING

Preparation Grading and soil preparation are the same as for seeding, with one exception. There is no need to develop a fine seed bed. Simply rake and cross rake until the required surface levels are achieved, and the soil is fine enough to bed the sod in intimate contact with the soil surface.

Purchasing Sod should contain hardy kinds of grasses that are known to produce good quality lawns in the region. Grasses should be healthy, vigorous, dense, medium to dark green in colour and mowed to the correct height. The sod should exhibit plenty of healthy, moist roots and good tensile strength, holding together easily when unrolled and shaken. It will be uniform, 1 1/4 to 1 1/2 inch (3-3.75 cm) thick, free from weeds, quack grass, other rogue or weed grasses and pests and diseases.

LAYING

The sod should be kept in the shade to prevent it from drying out. Cover it with damp burlap if the weather is warm. Do not cover with plastic. It causes too much heat when the sun is on it. Lay the sod as soon after delivery as possible.

Starting at one end of the area to be sodded, lay a row of sod across the area and several feet up the sides. Place a wide plank on the first row of sod.

Standing on the plank, facing the bare, undisturbed prepared soil, lay the next row of sod in front of the plank. Flip the plank forward onto the second row of sod and stand on it. Lay the next row of sod and continue the procedure until the entire area is covered. This method avoids standing on the soil to be sodded and all of the associated compaction, raking and re-raking that many unreflective gardeners go through.

Here are a few additional suggestions when laying sod:
- lay the sod one inch (2.5 cm) beyond the final margins of the lawn area to permit cutting back to form a clean, sharp edge after the sod has knitted.
- lightly pat the sod to ensure contact with the soil surface; standing on the plank will ensure intimate contact.
- lay the sod in a brickwork-like pattern, breaking all joints.
- tightly butt each sod up to its neighbours.
- using a sharp knife, cut out any weeds and plug the resulting holes with sod or soil.
- to transport sods to the area being sodded, place planks across the laid sod to the laying plank. Use a wheelbarrow to carry the sods. Place the rolled sods on the bare soil just in front of the laying plank.
- it is not necessary to roll the sod after laying.
- water frequently after laying the sod to maintain it in a moist but not soggy condition. When the sod has knitted and is beginning to grow, reduce the frequency and increase the volume of watering.
- when the grass has grown about three inches (7.5 cm) high, begin routine cutting and maintenance.
- after the sod is well knitted and growing, a light rolling may be given but is not necessary.

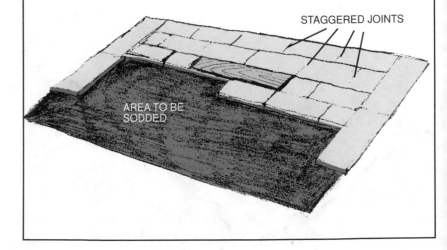

STAGGERED JOINTS

AREA TO BE SODDED

If your objective is a lush, green, hard wearing, uniformly textured, self-healing, beautiful lawn, a routine lawn maintenance program is essential. This is not to say that a reasonable lawn can't result from a less than comprehensive program. Only you can set an acceptable standard.

MOWING

Mowing is a most important operation that strongly affects the quality, health, vigour and longevity of a lawn.

Height of Cut Unlike most other plants, the region of active growth and elongation on grasses is near ground level, rather than at the tips of shoots. To avoid cutting off these regions of growth, it is necessary to cut at the right height above ground level.

Alternate mowing directions each time the grass is cut to help maintain an even looking surface.

Height of cut is measured by placing the mower on a hard, level surface and measuring the distance between the cutting blade or bed bar and the hard surface.

Cutting at the right height is most important, since it

- increases the rate of growth and the vigour of shoots and leaves
- improves the self healing properties of the lawn
- increases the density of shoots and leaves
- reduces the width of leaf blades, resulting in a finer textured lawn
- stimulates a more succulent, lush, vigorous growth of leaves

The correct height of cut for the Vancouver region is one to two inches (2.5 to 5 cm).

Frequency Failing to cut often enough is a common cause of poor quality lawns. They should be cut

- every 3-4 days during the flush of early growth in spring and early summer
- every 5-7 days during summer — perhaps a bit less often when the weather is very hot
- once in 10-14 days as the weather cools and growth slows in the fall

As a general rule of thumb, don't allow more than two inches (five cm) of new growth to develop between cuts.

In the early spring and when the weather is hot and dry raise the height of the mower to two inches (five cm) if your normal cutting height is one inch (2.5 cm) so that the grass is not cut too short.

Do not cut when the grass is wet unless really necessary.

It is not necessary to remove the clippings unless the grass is very long. Short clippings will decompose and return nutrients to the soil.

If you go on vacation and the grass gets long between cuts, cut it first at three to four inches (7.5 to 10 cm) high. Reduce the height of cut by 1/2 to 3/4 inch (1.25 to 2 cm) on each subsequent cut until you are back to the regular cutting height.

Sharp Mower Maintain a sharp mower throughout the cutting season. Sharp cuts heal cleanly and quickly, resulting in quick recovery and fast subsequent growth. Ragged cuts result in slow healing and recovery. They also give the lawn a brownish cast.

FERTILIZING

For general information about fertilizers, see Chapter 3.

A regular program is needed on lawns. Ideally, one pound (2.2 kg) per month of nitrogen, such as 20-9-5, in mid-May, mid-June, early September and November after the grass is dormant. The fall application should have slow release fertilizer, 3-5-20 or 3-6-36. If only one or two applications are made they should be in early May or early September. Three applications could be made with one in late May and the second and third in the fall in September and November. One of the late fall applications should be a complete fertilizer.

Caution should be exercised after mid-August. Late fertilizing with lots of nitrogen, especially if warm temperatures prevail for several weeks, can stimulate late growth that may be damaged by fall frosts and affect the winter hardiness of the lawn. Knowledge of local conditions and practices are the best guidelines.

To calculate the weight of a specific fertilizer to provide one pound (2.2 kg) of N, divide 100 by the percentage of N the fertilizer contains. Using 16-20-0 as an example, 100 / 16 = 6.25 lbs. (2.8 kg)in other words, 6.25 lbs. (2.8 kg) of 16-20-0 fertilizer will supply one pound (.45 kg) of actual nitrogen.

Professional Ratios Professional greens keepers at golf courses and sports-grounds have developed preferences for certain fertilizer ratios.

Bear in mind that ratios are not the same as percentages. For example fertilizers with percentages 1-2-3, 2-4-6, 3-6-9, and 4-8-12, are all examples (multiples) of the ratio 1:2:3.

Some ratios preferred by professional greens-keepers include:

4:1:2, 3:1:2, 2:1:1, 4:1:1, and 5:1:2. Even though there is some variation relative to P and K, the N is relatively high in most ratios.

Technique Here are a few fundamentals to help ensure the proper application of fertilizers:

- calculate and measure the amount of fertilizer needed.
- apply the fertilizer evenly and uniformly to promote an even rate of growth and uniform colour. This may be achieved by using the methods described for seeding.

> **To avoid burning the grass**
> - **don't overlap or dump in piles**
> - **don't apply to wet grass**
> - **do apply to dry grass**
> - **do "water in" immediately after applying**

WATERING

As a rule of thumb, during the growing season lawns need one inch (2.5 cm) of water every 7-10 days. This may be supplied naturally, artificially or, more often, by a combination of both. A good watering will penetrate at least nine inches (22.5 cm) deep. For watering established lawns the general rule applies — water copiously and deeply when required, leaving as long a period as practical between waterings.

Use a good quality sprinkler that produces a reasonably fine droplet and a has slow rate of application to ensure deep watering without puddling and loss by run-off.

To measure the rate of application, place several tin cans on the grass within the spread of the sprinkler to be tested. Turn on the water. When the water in the bottom of a can is one inch (2.5 cm) deep, that particular spot around the can has received one inch (2.5 cm) of water. This method indicates any variations in volume at several points under the sprinkler. It also allows for the calculation of how long it takes for a particular sprinkler to apply one inch of water.

> **Remember that frequent, shallow watering encourages the development of weeds, moss and shallow rooted grass plants susceptible to drought.**

Indicators Signs that watering is needed include
- dry surface soil, 1/2 to 3/4 inches (1.25 to 2 cm) deep.
- wilting grass leaves
- leaves turning a darker green colour, especially in varieties of Kentucky Bluegrass

WEED CONTROL

The development of a healthy, lush and dense lawn through a sound, maintenance program is the primary means to prevent weeds from becoming established. Inevitably, however, a few will still get into the lawn.

Where only a few weeds are involved, hand picking and spot treatments may be all that are needed. Watering a day or two before hand picking will soften the soil, making the job easier. Be sure to pull or dig up as much root as possible.

Raking prior to mowing helps to tear out creeping kinds and sets up weed foliage ready for the mower.

Correct watering practices also help to reduce weeds, especially the establishment of weed seedlings.

Where necessary, spot treatments or general spraying using chemicals may be carried out.

Chemical Control   Most lawn herbicides contain plant hormones. These are absorbed through the leaves of weeds, move throughout the plant and slowly cause grossly distorted growth. In a sense the plant grows itself to death.

Bear in mind that, basically, they kill only broad leaved weeds. Apart from Creeping Bent grasses, which they can damage, lawn herbicides don't kill lawn grasses. This is why they are known as "selective" herbicides. Also remember that they can kill or at best seriously damage all broad-leaved, woody and herbaceous plants. So use with them great care!

Commonly used, selective herbicides include:
- 2,4-D amine: used to control dandelion, broadleaf plantain and many other broad leaved weeds. Not as effective in controlling clover and chickweed, although repeated applications can take their toll of these two invasive weeds.
- Mecoprop: used against broadleaf plantain, chickweed, ground ivy, prostrate knotweed and white clover.
- Dicamba: used to control Prostrate Knotweed and White Clover.

The "Clover and Chickweed Killers," containing a mixture of 2,4-D, Mecoprop and Dicamba are very effective general lawn herbicides that will kill a broad spectrum of lawn weeds

Application   When applying these herbicides, the following practices are suggested:
- follow exactly the manufacturer's directions on the package.
- don't be tempted to use stronger than recommended spray solutions. Remember, a slow kill is the best response.
- spray on a warm, still, dry day when the temperature is above 70° F (22° C) and below 80° F (27° C) and the wind speed is less than 4 m.p.h. (6.5 km.p.h.).
- ideally the soil should be moist and the weeds growing vigorously.
- fertilizing a week ahead will stimulate weed growth and improve herbicide effectiveness.
- use low pressure in the sprayer to minimize the problem of drifting.

- keep the spray directed downward and close to the lawn.
- apply evenly and don't miss any weeds.
- if it rains within 24 hours of spraying, it may be necessary to re-spray.
- don't allow any spray to drift onto plants located adjacent to the lawn. If in doubt, wash bordering plants with water, immediately after spraying. To protect plants, cover them with paper or plastic prior to spraying.
- after spraying, wash out the sprayer with detergent and rinse three times with clean water.
- keep weed control chemicals in tightly closed, well labelled containers under lock and key.
- don't store herbicides with live plants or fertilizers. Several fertilizers are deliquescent and absorb herbicide fumes.
- to be really on the safe side, use separate sprayers for herbicides and other pesticides.
- during spraying, keep the spray away from your face and bare skin. Wear a long-sleeved shirt and long pants. Don't inhale the spray. A mask should be worn over the nose and mouth when chemicals are being sprayed. Wash all exposed skin or (better still) take a shower after spraying.

Herbicide impregnated wax weed bars are also effective and easy to use. For best effect the temperature should be above 70° F (22° C), but not too hot. Check the label for maximum temperature. Simply drag the bar slowly and deliberately over the lawn, slightly overlapping each strip covered to make sure that coverage is complete.

> - **Herbicide treated grass cannot be used for mulching and should not be added to the compost pile for three mowings after the herbicide has been used.**
> - **Keep children and pets off the lawn after it has been treated with herbicide until the odour is no longer evident.**

Quack Grass Using glyphosphate, it is possible to get rid of this invasive, weed grass in an existing lawn.

There are two approaches:
- spray the infested patches of lawn, killing both quack and lawn grasses. Then about one week later, seed or sod the resulting bare spots, or
- first, let the quack grass grow three or four inches (7.5 to 10 cm) above the tops of the lawn grasses. Very carefully apply a solution

of glyphosate to the tips of the quack grass only. Use a soft brush or cloth-wrapped piece of wood. Be sure not to drip one iota on the lawn grasses. Special applicators that look like hockey sticks are available in garden centres.

Crabgrass and Annual Bluegrass   These lawn weeds are difficult to control because they are annual weeds that spread by seed. Healthy thick lawn grass is your best defence for keeping these weeds out of the lawn. There are several pre-emergent herbicides available at garden shops which should be applied in the fall or early spring before the seeds germinate.

MOSS

Moss is a common problem on the coast. If the conditions are right it will invade the lawn. A healthy lawn will not be invaded as easily as a lawn with poor growing conditions such as too much shade, poor drainage or acidic soil conditions.

Moss killer applied according to the manufacturer's directions will kill the moss, which is then raked out of the lawn. Over-seed the bare areas left after the moss is removed.

Unless the initial cause is corrected, the moss will re-invade the lawn.

RAKING

Thatch is the build up of dead grass parts at the soil surface which happens if the material is not breaking down naturally faster than it is accumulating. If if accumulates more than 1/2 inch (1.25 cm), it should be removed. If the lawn is well drained and not over-watered or over-fertilized the thatch will not build up. But when it has accumulated it needs to be removed. Rent a vertical mower designed to do the job unless the area is small. Then a good raking will do the job. De-thatch the lawn in the early spring or early fall. Rake up the dead grass. Water and fertilize the grass. A word of warning: the lawn will look pretty awful for a few weeks until the new growth has taken over so don't plan a garden party right after you have de-thatched the lawn.

SCARIFYING

This is the practice of shallow raking to loosen just the soil surface of a lawn. A hand rake or vertical cutting power mower may be used. It is carried out when over-seeding a lawn.

It is also used frequently on bentgrass golf and bowling greens to sever over-ground runners prior to top dressing - - a practice seldom seen in the average home garden.

AERIFYING

Aerifying is the practice of making slits or narrow holes in the top few inches of a lawn. The basic purpose is to relieve soil compaction on heavily-used lawns. The resultant slits or holes shatter the soil a little, allowing easier penetration of air, water and fertilizer. Aerifying improves surface drainage, reduces surface run off and improves root development. The release of trapped carbon dioxide and toxic gases is also facilitated.

Slicing is easily and quickly carried out. Since it disturbs the lawn surface only slightly, it does not interfere with normal lawn maintenance.

Hollow tine aerifying results in small, narrow holes in the lawn and lifts small cores of soil, laying them on the lawn surface. These cores are then broken up and scattered by raking or dragging a flexible steel doormat over the lawn. Ideally the cores should be raked up and removed, followed by top dressing and fertilizing.

Aerifying may be carried out any time during the growing season, preferably a day or two following a heavy rain or watering when the ground is soft and easily penetrated.

Appropriate equipment is easily rented or a contractor may be hired.

TOP DRESSING

The application of soil, organic matter and sand or mixtures of these materials to a lawn surface is called top dressing. The purposes of this practice are to

- help to control thatch by accelerating natural decomposition.
- level a lawn surface by filling in minor hollows
- improve the drainage and texture of the soil surface
- encourage grass plants to produce more tillers or basal shoots, thereby increasing density
- serve as a mild fertilizer
- act as a carrier for concentrated fertilizers
- follow hollow-tine aerifying, to improve the soil structure and fertility
- provide a measure of winter protection in cold climates

On a level, well constructed, well maintained, vigorous lawn, top dressing will seldom be needed. However, it is not likely to do any harm if properly done.

For general purposes, a mix of four parts medium loam, one part sphagnum peat moss and one part coarse, gritty sand is satisfactory. It should be passed through a 3/8 inch (one cm) screen to remove lumps and stones. Ideally, a top dressing compost should be similar in composition to the underlying lawn soil.

Before applying, cut the grass. Use 1/8 to 3/4 cu. yd. per 1000 sq. ft. (0.16 to 0.98 m³ per 930 m²) of lawn area, spreading it evenly over the lawn. A rule of thumb is never to apply more than 1/4 inch (0.6 cm) deep layer at lawn soil level per application. Deeper layers can cause the grass to rot and may asphyxiate the grass plants. Using a stiff broom, back of a rake or drag mat, work the top dressing down between the grass blades to the soil surface level.

There is seldom any need to apply sand or organic matter alone. Sharp sand may improve surface drainage on clay soils. A very light dressing of well rotted, crumbly, finely-broken manure can provide a mild stimulant, especially when applied after hollow-tine aerifying.

ROLLING

The only justification for this practice is to settle a lawn surface that may have heaved after a hard, frosty winter. Its use is to be discouraged in maintaining home lawns.

RENOVATION

Before considering renovation, check the depth and condition of the top soil. If it's not adequate to support a good lawn, reconstruction is indicated.

Here is a sequence of steps to follow when renovating a lawn:

- spray with a selective, lawn herbicide to eliminate all weeds.
- cut the grass, about one inch (2.5 cm) high.
- thoroughly rake to remove all thatch.
- hollow tine aerify and remove all cores.
- top dress with a general compost.
- apply 10-30-10 or similar fertilizer at 10 lbs per 1000 sq. ft. (4.5 kg per 930 m^2) of lawn surface area.
- water the lawn copiously.
- follow up with a full, routine maintenance program.

CHAPTER 10

PESTS & DISEASES

While a few, mostly small, mammals cause damage to plants, the majority of garden pests are insects and mites, plus a few molluscs and eelworms. Additionally, several fungi, bacteria and viruses cause diseases in plants.

The common classes of pests and diseases and brief descriptions of their general life cycles are discussed in this chapter.

OFFENDERS AND LIFE CYCLES

INSECTS

Most insects hatch from eggs laid by mature adults, emerging as larvae (caterpillars, worms and slug-worms, etc.). The larvae feed on the leaves, flowers, shoots, buds, and roots of their host plants. When fully developed, they are transformed into pupae or chrysalids which become quiescent, resting for a time. Finally, adults emerge from the pupae to feed, mate and reproduce — repeating the cycle. While there are many variations in life cycles, this description serves as a general model.

MITES

Mites are related to the true spiders but don't have clearly defined body segments. They have six legs when young and eight when adult. Mites are generally much smaller than spiders. The common red spider mite can't be easily seen with the naked eye. Their life styles are extremely diverse. From the gardener's point of view, all stages except eggs cause damage to plants, in some cases extensively.

NEMATODES OR EELWORMS

Eelworms are minute, often microscopic, worm-like creatures, tapering towards both ends. Young and mature forms cause damage by burrowing into and living within the various organs of their hosts.

FUNGI

Fungus diseases usually begin their life cycles as spores. These are similar to seeds in flowering plants. Spores sprout or germinate on leaves, shoots and roots etc., producing minute, thread-like growths that either run over the surface of the affected leaf or shoot or, after penetration, inside the plant tissues. They go through an often complicated life cycle, finally producing adult spore bearing bodies which repeat the cycle.

BACTERIA

Bacteria infect plants as spores or live cells. They don't develop thread-like growths like fungi, although some kinds produce chains of cells. Usually they are single celled, growing and multiplying within the body of the host plant, usually gaining entry through wounds or natural openings in the plant. They cannot penetrate a plant's cuticle or skin.

Most fungal and bacterial diseases are parasitic, the invading organism being dependent on the host for its survival.

VIRUSES

Viruses are sub-microscopic organisms that invade the plant's cells, interfering with the nucleus, other microscopic organs, and metabolism. They can only multiply and survive inside the plant, often killing the host. Viruses are infectious and often transmitted by sucking insects. They may also be spread by pruning and handling plants.

There are no dependable chemical controls for viruses.

OFFENDERS AND SYMPTOMS

INSECTS

The type of damage depends on the feeding habits of the particular insect. Here are the most common kinds:

Sucking   These kinds have needle-like, piercing mouthparts called stylets. They push them into leaves and shoots, sucking out the sap. Sometimes at the same time, they inject a digestive enzyme. This results in a small hole and causes irritation. The plant responds with puckered leaves and distorted growth, particularly at the tender growing tips of shoots and in opening buds and unfurling leaves. Aphids, which are often called greenfly or blackfly, and other plant lice, leaf hoppers and red spider mites are examples.

Biting and Chewing   Leaves and tender shoots are bitten into and pieces, removed and/or eaten. Typical symptoms are irregular and scallop-shaped leaf margins, totally skeletonized leaves, entire leaves eaten, pieces chewed out of shoots and distorted growing tips on new shoots. Prime examples include caterpillars of all kinds, weevils and several beetles.

Rasping   Some insects and molluscs have rough, sandpaper-like mouthparts. They feed by scraping off the leaf surfaces, leaving obvious open patches and sometimes semi-to fully- skeletonized areas. As these areas dry out, they may turn brownish. Slugs and pear slugs (sawfly larvae) are examples.

Mining Leaf miners lay eggs in between the upper and lower leaf surfaces. The eggs hatch and the larvae tunnel through the leaves eating the soft tissues. Characteristic damage is meandering, whitish lines or irregularly-shaped patches. When patches dry out, they become papery textured and brownish. Birch, lilac, columbine and beet leaf miners are common.

Leaf Rolling ,Curling and Sticking Leaves are rolled, puckered or formed into pockets, stuck together with sticky substances or silk-like threads, forming a protective hiding place for larvae and pupae. Aphids and many leaf rolling caterpillars are typical.

MOLLUSCS

These are represented by slugs and snails. Slimy silvery trails of mucus and rasped foliage are the main symptoms.

NEMATODES

These tiny creatures enter the plant tissues, where they multiply. General symptoms are distorted growth of leaves, shoots, flowers, bulbs, buds and roots, depending on the characteristics of the eelworm species and host plant. Some cause cysts on roots and others stimulate the growth of galls on shoots. Many kinds are difficult to control.

DISEASES

Symptoms of both *fungal* and *bacterial* diseases include
- shoot and root blight — sudden browning or blackening of leaves and young shoots, and curled, shoot tips
- wefts of whitish or greyish fungal threads on leaves, young shoots and shoot tips
- spots on leaves and fruits
- raised or depressed cankers or lesions on stems,
- fruit rot
- wilting of a part or an entire plant
- galls close to the crown, at or just above the soil level
- shoot or root rot

Symptoms of *virus* diseases include
- distorted growth of leaves, stems and flowers
- various shaped patterns of yellow, pale green and green on the leaves, often superficially resembling mosaics
- stunted growth and smaller-than-normal leaves
- yellowing between the leaf veins
- pale-coloured to transparent veins on leaves
- general unthrifty growth

CONTROL

Effective control involves regular inspection, identification of the problem and the selection of the appropriate control method.

REGULAR INSPECTION

The first line of defence is regular inspection. The time to take control action is when the first few bugs or spots are noticed — not when the infestation has reached epidemic proportions.

Check every plant in the garden every week. Learn to recognize the early warning symptoms — a half rolled leaf, a growing tip just a bit off centre or slightly twisted, one or two aphids or caterpillars, a dull sheen on leaves or a few leaves at an unnatural angle. By learning to recognize the signs of normal, healthy growth, you will be quick to notice deviations.

Good gardeners learn to recognize problems from fifty paces.

IDENTIFY THE PROBLEM

This is the next step. Make sure that you know the problem, in order to select the proper control method. It comprises two integrated parts:

- observe and identify the pest or disease on the plant, by noting its size, shape, colour and other characteristics, and
- describe the damage or symptoms.

DECIDE THE CONTROL

The final step, which always follows and never precedes the first, is to determine the appropriate method of control. It's a bad practice to jump to conclusions about pest control, especially when chemical methods are to be used.

CONTROL METHODS

There are two basic approaches to control: non-chemical or cultural, and chemical, both of which are discussed below.

NON-CHEMICAL

Healthy, strong, vigorous, well-grown plants in their proper environment are not as susceptible to pests and diseases as those which are neglected and weak or grown in the wrong environment. Even when attacked, well-grown plants withstand the onslaught and recover much better. The first line of attack is, therefore, defence, by providing optimum cultural conditions and practices.

General Sanitation   Pick up and dispose of litter and rubbish that gets trapped and accumulates in corners and along the base of fences and hedges, etc. Hoe regularly with a dutch hoe to eliminate weeds and stir the soil surface to disturb insect eggs, larvae and adults. Remove boards and flat stones that can provide a refuge for slugs and beetles or use them as a trap. Lift the boards often and remove the pests hidden there. Be circumspect about piles of firewood — they can act as home to many insects. Keep the garden clean at all times.

Digging and Forking Every fall, dig over all vegetable plots and flower beds and borders, exposing the soil to the cleansing effect of winter weather. Fork as deeply as practical between established shrubs and herbaceous perennials, short of seriously disturbing their root systems, leaving the soil as level as possible between plants.

Spacing Plants Don't place plants closer than necessary to achieve the desired effect or objective.

Hand Picking Although some people are a bit squeamish about this method, when insect populations are small it's effective and practical. Pick off the bugs and, if you can't abide the thought of squashing them underfoot, drop them into a jar of soapy water to be flushed down the toilet later.

Trapping Night feeders, including slugs, may be trapped by providing cool, moist hiding places during the day. Flat stones, boards, citrus fruit and cucumber peel, and the leaves of lettuce and cabbage may be laid on the ground. Lift them during the day and destroy the hiding bugs. Cockroaches, slugs and some other beetles are attracted to beer. Sink a small can or jar of beer in the ground up to its rim. Bugs attracted by the smell will investigate, fall in and drown.

Washing Regular, reasonably forceful spraying with water will keep many pests at bay. Mites in particular do not like water or high humidity. The spray will knock off many bugs and eggs, preventing them from establishing a beachhead. It also keeps foliage clean, optimizing photosynthesis.

Soapy water One tbsp. (15 mL) of pure soap to one quart (one L) of water will provide a measure of control of many pests, particularly the soft-bodied kinds like aphids, leaf hoppers and some caterpillars. An old remedy is one pound (2.2 kg) of high grade, non-caustic, soft-soap, thoroughly mixed with 10 gallons (45 L) of water. Be careful with plants that have a waxy, bluish or glaucous skin or cuticle such as carnations, pinks and some conifers. The soap solution may melt the wax and discolour the foliage. If in doubt, first test one stem or leaf.

Insecticidal soaps can also be used. They are very popular with environmentally-conscious gardeners.

Working and harvesting Don't work among or harvest plants when foliage is wet.

Avoid breaking, bruising or otherwise damaging plants when walking or working among them.

Removal of plants Remove and destroy plants infected by viruses and those seriously affected by blights and wilts.

Any plant which is infected by any disease to the point where growth is stunted and badly distorted should be considered for discarding.

Pruning   Remove broken, physically damaged, badly diseased and dead stems, shoots and branches from all plants as noticed. Cut back into healthy tissue just above and slightly sloping back from a bud or side shoot that is pointing away from the centre of the plant.

Discoloured foliage   Pick and destroy discoloured and dead leaves from plants and the soil surface.

Watering and spraying   Avoid over-watering. Frequent watering keeps the soil surface moist and can create very high humidity, particularly during naturally humid periods.

Spray with water when the atmosphere is buoyant and moving, not when the weather is dull, overcast and sultry.

Avoid over-fertilizing, which leads to soft weak growth that is prone to insect and disease.

CHEMICAL

There are many effective pesticides. New kinds are being developed each year. The use of chemicals in the home garden is regulated by the Federal and Provincial governments through their departments of Agriculture and Fisheries.

These bodies approve the kinds of chemicals suitable for home use, specific formulations and methods of application.

In general, pesticides fall within the following categories:

Contact Insecticides   These chemicals kill insects on contact or soon thereafter. They may directly hit the insect or it may pick up the chemical on its feet. Many modern insecticides are in this category. Several commonly-used kinds are only persistent for 24-48 hours, breaking down to harmless compounds. With serious problems, repeat spraying may be necessary.

Useful in controlling sucking and biting insects.

Stomach Poisons   These coat the leaves with insecticide which is ingested by the insect during feeding.

Used to control biting and chewing insects.

Systemic Insecticides   This type is absorbed by the plant through its leaves and soft stems, and distributed via the sap stream throughout the plant. It is absorbed by the insect during feeding regardless of the pest's location on or within the plant and its method of feeding. Since systemics stay inside the plant for a while, they are effective over a longer period than contact insecticides.

They are used to control hard-to-hit pests such as leaf miners, leaf rollers, leaf curling aphids and persistent repeaters.

Fumigants   These chemicals generate gases or fumes. Most commonly used to control pests in greenhouses, where the fumes can be confined, and soil borne pests. Seldom used by home gardeners, except as a contracted service.

Contact Fungicides These kill or check the development of fungus diseases on the outside of the plant.

Systemic Fungicides Absorbed by the plant and distributed throughout the sap stream, these kinds kill or check both external and internal fungus diseases.

Bactericides As the name implies, these chemicals control bacteria. Since many bacteria are hard to control, there are not too many control chemicals. Copper oxychloride formulations are among the commonest. Old fashioned Bordeaux mixture is still used to control some blights. It is made by mixing one part copper sulphate and one part calcium hydroxide in one hundred parts of clean water. If this mix causes foliage burning, reduce the copper sulphate up to one half.

APPLICATION METHODS

Bearing in mind the comments regarding taking action before a problem reaches epidemic proportions, spot treatments are a good form of control. Rather than dousing the entire garden or even an entire plant, treat only the affected areas, plants or parts, if the problem can be isolated.

This will not always be possible. For example, when applying systemic insecticides, full coverage of a plant is required to get enough pesticide into the sap stream, or when you are uncertain of the extent of an infestation.

Bear in mind that an inadequate level of control is also undesirable since it leads to unnecessary duplication of control measures.

Spraying The pesticide is thoroughly mixed with water and, in some applications, a spreader-sticker or wetting agent (surfactant). Using a pneumatic or pump action sprayer, this mixture is sprayed on the affected plant.

A high-pressure spray, producing a fine droplet, misty spray is best.

There are several formulations. Emulsifiable concentrates mix readily with water, staying in suspension. On the other hand, wettable powders require continual agitation during spraying.

The first two rules of spraying are "read the label," and "follow, exactly, the manufacturer's or supplier's directions."

The basic spraying technique is to completely cover both sides of the leaves and all stems. Start at the base of the plant with the spray nozzle directed up and work upward, finishing at the top.

Dusting Pesticides are mixed with fine particle carriers and dusted onto the plants. It's not easy to get dusts on the undersides of leaves. On the other hand, they are easy to apply to the soil.

Dusts are best applied during still, humid weather. Try to create clouds of dust that drift among the leaves. An old method is to put the powder in a nylon stocking and gently tap it with a piece of wood. Bellows-operated dusting machines are available.

Granules   Several pesticides for the control of soil pests are available in granular form. These are broadcast over the soil surface, applied in the bottom of or alongside a seed drill or worked into the soil.

Drenches   These are liquid formulations applied to the soil as a drench. They may be systemic pesticides absorbed through plant roots rather than leaves, or non-systemic, aimed at a soil borne pest or disease.

SAFETY

When spraying, here are some safety precautions:

- to avoid drifting sprays, don't spray when it's too windy.
- always stand on the windward side to avoid spraying yourself.
- don't spray other people or their plants.
- when spraying, wear long-sleeved shirts and long pants, as well as a mask which covers the nose and mouth.
- spray when the temperature is above 70° F(22° C) but not over 80° F (26° C).
- avoid spraying during strong, direct sunlight, especially when the temperature is over 80° F (26° C).
- after spraying, wash all exposed skin, or better still, take a shower.
- shoot a half container of clean water through the sprayer after spraying to flush out and clean the spray head, pipes and tubes, and rinse out the sprayer a couple of times.
- hang the sprayer upside down to drain, and, if made of metal, to prevent rusting. The modern, high quality, plastic sprayers are not plagued with rust problems and are efficient.
- make sure all pesticides are well capped and clearly labelled. Store them in a cool, shaded place under lock and key, out of the reach of children.

COMMON PESTS AND DISEASES IN VANCOUVER

There are many insect pests that are bad some years but not others. These include cutworms, earwigs, flea beetles and various maggots. Treat these as they appear. UBC Botanical Gardens and Van Dusen Botanical Gardens both have Hort Lines which dispense gardening advice.

APHIDS

Aphids are the most common pests in Vancouver. They come in many colours: black, pink, grey and the most common, green. They are sap sucking insects which quickly form colonies, usually on the young foliage. They can also spread virus diseases from plant to plant. They have a complicated life cycle and produce several generations over the summer which for the most part are wingless females. They over-winter on alternate hosts — usually weeds.

Control aphids as soon as spotted to prevent them from increasing. Water from the hose, soapy water or rubbing them off by hand works well. If the infestation is very bad, suitable chemicals are available.

SLUGS

Slugs and snails are always a concern when you live in a high rainfall area. They are not insects but molluscs. They can nibble on a plant or devour it in one sitting, depending on their size. Check the grass and garden early in the morning and in the cool of the evening, and destroy them. Commercial baits are available. They should be used with care so children and pets cannot get at them.

SCALE

Scale seems to be ever-present in Vancouver. When the infestations are bad, the streets and cars under infected trees glisten with honey dew. They are not easy to control, particularly on large trees. An insecticide is sprayed in June or July, depending on the type of scale, when the eggs have hatched and the tiny crawlers are unprotected by the scale.

WEEVILS

Weevils of different species attack rhododendrons, strawberries and many ornamentals. They chew holes along the edges of the leaves and damage the fruit. The larva damages the roots of many ornamentals.

Control at night, using a flashlight and hand-picking the adults, or set traps of rolled up newspaper. There is a new control available which employs nematodes to kill the larva. The nematodes will not damage plants.

CRANE FLIES OR LEATHER JACKETS

Crane Flies or Leather Jackets in lawns are always a concern because the adult looks like a monster mosquito. Unless there was a lot of damage the year before there is usually not too much need for concern. They cause irregular brown patches on the lawn. They can also be a problem in the flower and vegetable garden.

If they were bad the previous year or if there are more than 20 maggots per 100 m² (1076 sq.ft.), spray with an insecticide in May.

CABBAGE LOOPERS

Cabbage Loopers are green caterpillars with a thin white stripe on either side of their bodies. They like to dine on any of the cabbage family as well as celery, beets, peas and spinach, chewing holes in the leaves. Adults are grey moths. There are several generations over the summer.

Control by hand-picking the larva or cover the crops with a cloth like Reemay. A biological control called *Bacillus thuringiensis* (B.T.) is a bacteria which only kills caterpillars.

IMPORTED CABBAGE WORM

This is the larva of the pretty greenish-white butterfly that flutters around the garden in the summer. It makes holes in the brassicas as well as turnips and radishes. There are several generations over the summer.

Control is the same as for the cabbage looper.

DISEASES

POWDERY MILDEW

It is very prevalent in Vancouver, particularly on roses, although it is not restricted to them. It looks like the leaves are covered with greyish-white powder.

Control by spraying the plants with lime sulphur during the dormant season. Destroy all leaves in the fall. Washing the leaves down with water helps to control the mildew by breaking down its delicate structure. Fungicides can be used every two weeks during the spring and early summer.

BLACK SPOT

Black spot, which is self-descriptive, is common on roses in Vancouver.

Control is achieved by setting up a spraying schedule with the fungicide Funginex. Spraying must be started early before there is any sign of the disease. Remove all leaves in the fall that are infected with the disease and destroy them.

RUST

Rust, which looks like reddish orange spots on the leaves, is common on many different plants, from roses to snapdragons.

Control is the same as for powdery mildew.

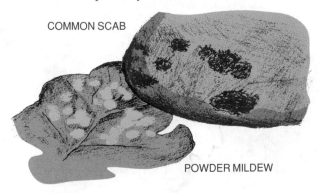

COMMON SCAB

POWDER MILDEW

FURTHER READING

Bubel, Nancy. *The New Seed Starters Handbook*. Pennsylvania: Rodale, 1988.

Carr, Anna. *Color Handbook of Garden Insects*. Emmaus: Rodale, 1979.

Newton, Judy.*The Complete Guide to Vegetables for Amateurs and Experts*. Vancouver: Whitecap, 1991.

Newton, Judy, and M. Garland, eds. *University of British Columbia Guide to Gardening in British Columbia*. Vancouver: U.B.C. Botanical Garden and Agricultural Sciences, 1990.

Phillips, Roger, and Martyn Rix. *Bulbs*. New York: Random House, 1989.

Phillips, Roger, and Martyn Rix. *Perennials*. 2 vols. New York: Random House, 1992.

Straley, Gerald B.*Trees of Vancouver*. Vancouver: U.B.C. Press, 1992.

Tarrant, David A. *Highrise Horticulture*. Vancouver: Whitecap, 1989.

Tarrant, David A. *Pacific Gardening Guide*. Vancouver: Whitecap, 1990.

Tarrant, David A. *Year in Your Garden*. Vancouver: Whitecap, 1989.

Taylor's Guide: Shrubs, Bulbs, Vegetables, Annuals, Groundcovers. Boston: Houghton Mifflin.

Judy Newton was born in Winnipeg, Manitoba, and moved to Vancouver in 1973 after living in California briefly. She has gardened most of her life, in all of these places. A member of the Davidson Club, Ms. Newton writes a monthly column in *Gardens West* magazine. She has authored *Hortline Questions and Answers*, published by U.B.C Botanical Gardens, and *The Complete Guide to Vegetables for Amateurs and Experts* (published in 1991). She was one of several authors of *University of British Columbia Guide to Gardening in British Columbia* (published in 1990), and was responsible for the technical co-ordination of this book. She received her B.Sc. in Agriculture with a specialization in Plant Science from U.B.C. in 1988 and presently works as an Education Assistant at the U.B.C Botanical Garden, where she arranges and teaches classes in gardening, conducts tours, and answers questions for the general public.

OTHER LONE PINE BOOKS FOR BRITISH COLUMBIA INCLUDE

British Columbia Wildlife Viewing Guide
Bill Wareham

Each description of sixty-seven of British Columbia's finest wildlife viewing sites is accompanied by information about available facilities, driving directions and an access map. Colour illustrations.

ISBN 1-55105-000-5 96 pp   5 1/2 x 8 1/2 $8.95

Birds of Victoria
Robin Bovey, Wayne Campbell and Bryan Gates

A beautifully illustrated, full colour guide to common birds found in and around Victoria. Ideal for the beginning or intermediate bird watcher. Colour illustrations.

ISBN 0-919433-75-8 144 pp   5 1/2 x 8 1/2 $9.95

Birds of Vancouver
Robin Bovey and Wayne Campbell

Informative and colourfully illustrated guide to the commonly found birds of Vancouver, intended for both the beginning and intermediate birder. Colour illustrations.

ISBN 0-919433-73-1 144 pp   5 1/2 x 8 1/2 $9.95

The Lone Pine Picnic Guide to British Columbia
Nancy Gibson and John Whittaker

A unique, entertaining guide to picnic spots throughout the province, with information on local history and things to see and do for each location, as well as interesting picnic menus and recipes. Illustrated, maps.

ISBN 0-919433-59-6 264 pp   5 1/2 x 8 1/ $11.95

Ski B.C.
Heather Doughty

A must for the avid skier. Includes descriptions of thirty-three of the best downhill ski areas in the province, including detailed hill maps. Also contains sections on heli-skiing, cat skiing, ski touring and cross-country skiing. Illustrated.

ISBN 0-919433-94-4 224 pp   5 1/2 x 8 1/2 $12.95

Look for these books at your local bookstore. If any unavailable, order direct from *Lone Pine Publishing,* 206,10426 - 81 Avenue, Edmonton, Alberta T6C 1X5

Phone: (403) 433-9333 or (604) 687-5555
Fax: (403) 433-9646 or (604) 687-5575